To my parents, Maria and Salvatore Leto.

To my husband, Adolph, and daughter, Maria.

Fashion Design for the Plus-Size

Fashion Design for the Plus-Size

Frances Leto Zangrillo

Associate Professor
Fashion Design—Apparel
Fashion Institute of Technology
New York

FAIRCHILD PUBLICATIONS
NEW YORK

The Color Box forecasts season's colors in a series of palettes and color combinations for inspiration with moveable yarn pompoms. Color combinations are illustrated on **cover** in a wool plaid fabric and printed design. The neutral printed fabric adds Color Box's "patio peach" as a tonal accent.

Elizabeth Valle, illustrator
Katharine Hulse, book designer

Standard Book Number: 87005-677-8

Library of Congress Catalog Card Number: 89-84198

Printed in the United States of America

Preface

Clothes must enhance. They must provide confidence and must be attractive to the individual no matter what the size may be, and today's woman comes in all sizes. She wants to wear clothes that are created for her and her lifestyle in designs that compliment and flatter her shape. Large-size women are hungry for clothes that will fit their ample figures. More large-size women today than in the past are philosophical and accept their dimensions. It's as if they are saying, "Why fight it, let's go out and enjoy life as we are."

Research I began in 1979 pointed to:

- Married women and mothers entering the work force in increasing numbers since the 1970s.

- Young women getting heavier for the last two decades.

In fact, 47 percent of American women, about 35 million, wear a size 14 or larger, and some 30 million American women weigh 160 pounds or more. For these women shopping has been a frustrating and depressing experience.

Large women comment: "I've never been able to buy a silk dress. All they make in my size is polyester." "I can't be the only size 20 who wants gabardine pants and cashmere sweaters." "I've missed a lot of social functions because I had nothing to wear and couldn't just go out and buy something off-the-rack." "Large-size dresses are matronly. I'm young—I want to dress like everyone else my age."

These are some of the complaints of the large-size women who are starting to talk back to manufacturers and stores that have been treating them as second class citizens. All they have been offered for years are polyester double knits, pants with elastic waistbands and acrylic bubble sweaters. Large-sized women relegated to flowered polyester are speaking out on style. They don't want shapeless A-line silhouettes in unattractive colors and prints. Large-size women are big news and bigger business these days.

As Curriculum Chairperson of the Fashion Design Department at the Fashion Institute of

Technology, I realized that this segment of the fashion world could not be ignored. Because of my conviction that our mission at F.I.T. is to bring forth people with a commitment to excellence and innovation, and with the support and assistance of my colleagues, a new course of study "Fashion Design for the Large and Petite Sizes" was introduced to our fashion design students. I taught this new course in the spring semester of 1980 and was confronted with the lack of a good and detailed text for designing plus sizes. This need has been the driving motivation behind my years of research and this text—*Fashion Design for the Plus-Size.*

Fashion Design for the Plus-Size describes the large-size market as challenging, productive and the segment of the apparel industry to be in. It is an invitation to engage in the challenge—to design the best-looking garments. The large-size woman is examined with reference to four major body silhouettes. You will learn how to emphasize the good body facts and de-emphasize the bad in your designs using the elements and principles of design as they apply to the plus-size woman. You will begin to think in terms of the total picture each body type presents. An exciting feature of my text is my interpretation of designs for the plus-size woman using designs from the collections of top American and European fashion designers.

Since a profile of the plus-size customer cannot be complete without demographic studies, I have included information on who is the full-figured woman—how old is she, what is her education, her income. Basic considerations are discussed regarding strategic business functions and how to determine the customer to target.

Fashion Design for the Plus-Size continues with a "how to" section including illustrations and detailed explanations of the basic principles of draping and drafting the various garments. The emphasis is on the draping principles and the "whys." Part Three includes five design interpretations utilizing the draped muslin slopers developed in Part Two. Part Four concludes this text with charts and diagrams covering grading for the plus-size as well as illustrations identifying the body proportions and how the body changes from one size to another.

The large woman was ignored by the fashion world for years and often became the forgotten woman. That is changing. What they want are the same clothes their chic sisters are wearing. In a word . . . fashion.

1990   Frances Leto Zangrillo
                                          New York

Acknowledgments

In appreciation for their cooperation and support I wish to thank:

- Bernard Zamkoff and Lillian D'Angelo, colleagues at F.I.T., for their support and assistance.

- Elizabeth Valle, my former student and very special friend, for her unending patience, creativity and skill in converting my photographs and rough drawings into the finished fashion illustrations you see throughout this text.

- Theresa Reilly, my colleague and friend, for her help with the initial drawings to meet my expectations of the plus-size figure.

- Lee White, who gave technical advice in photography when I draped each step of the draping projects discussed in this text.

- Leanne Epina and Joan Tobin, former photography students at F.I.T., who photographed the clothes from the Givenchy En Plus Collection.

- Jennene Booher of Maggy London, for her help and introduction to Kathleen McFetters, who generously supplied design sketches and information.

- Among those individuals and firms who graciously shared their information and material: Paul Biacomanno, Jose Caicado, The Color Box, Frank Egitto, Bernard Holtzman, Maureen Janoski, Arthur Kohler, Jeri Lambert, Lynn Montanno, Ellen Mullman, Albert Nipon, Inc., Jane Resnick, Ricky and William Smithline, Irving Solero, Dianne Specht, Ray Yules and the Wool Bureau.

- The Business of Plus-Sizes, a publication, for the many photographs they supplied for this text.

- Jim Bisciello, a good friend, for the introduction to Frank Philips of Leslie Fay Sports-

ACKNOWLEDGMENTS

wear II, who provided material, took time to answer all my questions and arranged for me to meet Armando De Benedictis.

- Armando De Benedictis for his helpful suggestions on the chapter on grading.

- Helen Genute, Givenchy En Plus, for providing the clothes that appear in the color insert.

- Jean Zeitlin, my sister, for her help in proofreading the manuscript.

- My husband, Adolph, and my daughter, Maria, for their patience and endurance.

- Fairchild Publications for their faith in *Fashion Design for the Plus-Size* and a special thank you to Olga Kontzias, my editor, for her genuine interest, talent, and contribution to this text.

Contents

CONTENTS

Fashion Design
for the Plus-Size

Part One

1 A Profile of the Plus-Size Figure

There is a bold new fashion world evolving for the size 16 plus woman. Manufacturers realize that big and beautiful is a lucrative and receptive market, which is encouraging the production of more and better wearing apparel and accessories for every activity.

The plus-size business is getting better as the image of the full-figured woman is being accepted. But it has taken a long time for the ready-to-wear manufacturer to develop fashionable clothing for this special customer. It has happened because America's obsession with thinness is waning. The National Center for Health Statistics reported that the total population has gotten plumper by six pounds from the 1960s to the 1980s. Despite all the exercise and nutritional awareness, people are getting bigger. The latest statistics state that 62 percent of women wear a size 12 or larger, 49 percent wear a size 14 or larger and 31 percent wear a size 16 or larger. Contrary to what has been believed for too long, large size women are young. Of the 31 percent who wear a size 16 or larger, 45 percent are 25 to 35 years old, and 35 percent are 35 to 50. By the year 2000 this market is expected to increase 60 percent.

The large woman wants to be glamorous. She has awakened to her fashion potential and has learned to make the most of her looks. She goes after beauty with an "I won't be denied" attitude. What a difference it has made to her when she is given the chance to wear something she really likes, something with style. There is no denying that people treat her differently when she looks good. And, of course, being treated better feeds her self-confidence. Large women represent an eight billion dollar market with projections to eighteen billion by the year 2000—no wonder more and more manufacturers are waking up to the challenge of designing for this market. It is quite gratifying for the manufacturer who can provide her with a fashionable outfit she can wear right out the door.

The designer and manufacturer who seize on the unique opportunities in this market need a profile of the plus-size woman, a knowledge of her lifestyle and most important, an understand-

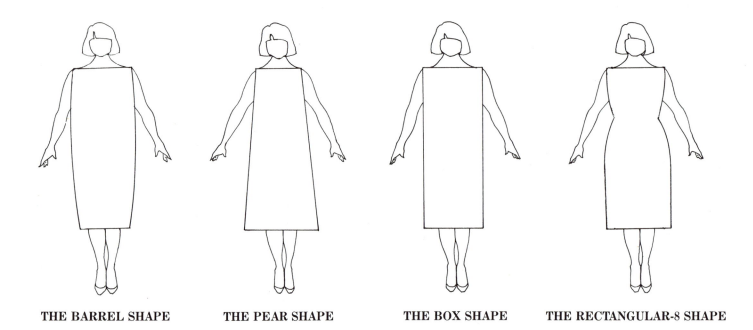

THE BARREL SHAPE   **THE PEAR SHAPE**   **THE BOX SHAPE**   **THE RECTANGULAR-8 SHAPE**

ing of her body proportions. Styling for the plus-size woman must consider her special needs. The plus-size woman must be accepted and a commitment made to give this customer the most flattering, comfortable and fashionable apparel possible.

Most important, and what makes the large-size woman look better, is good fit. Good fit means the large body needs darts, ease and tucks that will allow the fabric to skim over the contours, and drape gracefully without emphasizing them. Good fit has flattering proportions that shape the figure without confining or destroying it.

All large women are not large in the same area. Some women are large with small hips, some are large with small waists, others are large with small chests. Therefore, analyze the plus-size figure and identify the special body facts and failings, and match these into body silhouettes and height classifications. The full-figured woman cannot wear apparel that has been merely graded larger. A size 8 dress with shoulder pads and an emphasized bustline cannot just be sized up for a size 26. The scale of the design will be all wrong and will not fit the full figure comfortably. There are problems that need to be solved in styling from a missy size to a large size. Grading a missy size larger is one of the reasons why many manufacturers have been in and out of the large-size market (see **Part Four, Grading for the Plus-Size Figure**).

Body Types for the Plus-Size Woman

Full-figure body shapes have the same height proportions as their slimmer counterparts—average, petite and tall. Their body proportions can be divided into four major body silhouettes:

- The Rectangular-8 Shape

- The Pear Shape

- The Barrel Shape

- The Box Shape

Each silhouette suggests an overall contour of the body and how the body is proportioned and calls for a different fashion philosophy (which will be discussed in great detail). Once you understand the physical characteristics of each body type, you will be able to combine the line, design, fabric scale and colors to complement her special qualities. You will then create wonderful and unique combinations with style and flair that will reflect the image of your company and your creativity to this large-size customer.

The Rectangular-8 Shape

This body type is considered to be the most evenly proportioned. Nicely formed shoulders and gentle curves are in harmonious scale with the rest of the body (**Figure 1-1**). A rectangular-8 is formed if you start to outline the broad shoulders, sweep down around a full bust, to and across a slightly pinched waistline, over a proportionally round hip before reversing and returning to the shoulders. In most cases, the length of the legs equals the length of the torso; the arms are round and well proportioned. Almost any design will look well on this woman. Very few figure corrections are required. She dresses to project her personal style and not to change the proportions of her shape. The exception is when there is no waistline indentation. The rectangular-8 shape is popular with model agencies for the plus-size woman.

The Pear Shape

The pear-shape body type has a narrow top and usually a narrow shouldered torso that continues to the waist area, where it bells out over round hips or large bulging thighs (**Figure 1-2**). The wide hips do give the illusion of a small waistline. Many full round hip figures have small, full-cup breasts, full rounded upper arms and legs that taper to normal shapes from elbow to waist and knee to ankle. Some women with this body type have thin chests with hips or thighs curving out abruptly below small waists. And some have a stocky round torso with no waistline indentation. This figure type is most challenging and requires careful attention to style lines and silhouette in order to conceal the uneven proportions and bring them into balance.

The Barrel Shape

Women who fall into this body type tend to have a few physical blessings as well as some challenging flaws (**Figure 1-3**). The upper torso seems to be short but broader than the lower torso which translates into a short-waisted and wide-shouldered figure. In the profile this body type is profoundly top heavy, hence the term barrel-chested. The big problem here is the waist which is thicker in the middle than at the hips.

The Box Shape

This figure has a thick, short wide torso, wide hips and usually long legs with no visible waistline indentation (**Figure 1-4**). We can say this body type is fully firm and evenly packed, and appears to show little difference between shoulder, waist and hip measurements. Women with a box-shape figure are broad all around, straight up and down. They are enclosed by wide lines or tight angles. Curves just don't exist. The bust may be small or flat with broad shoulders. Big upper arms and legs taper to thick lower arms and calves with thick ankles. The box shape requires creating the illusion of a vertical silhouette. With this body silhouette you need to camouflage stockiness.

The large-size market is challenging, productive and, the segment of the apparel industry to be in. You have been given a likeness of the body proportions of the four major full-figure body silhouettes—the rectangular-8, pear, barrel and box shapes. A profile of the plus-size customer cannot be complete without demographic studies. Who is the full-figured woman? How old is she? What is her education, her income? How does she live? The answers are essential to complete the profile and to enter this market. The following chapter will discuss these basic considerations to determine the customer to target, how to know her lifestyle and how to develop an identity for your firm. These and strategic business functions will be examined in detail. You cannot be all things to all large-size consumers. The manufacturer with a marketing plan that knows their customers and satisfies her needs will emerge successful.

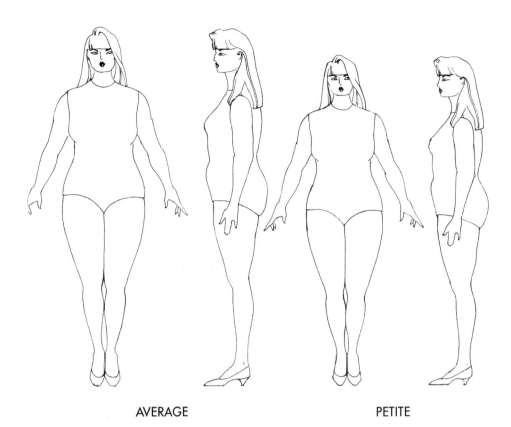

AVERAGE   PETITE

FIGURE 1-1   **Rectangular-8-shape Body Type**

AVERAGE   PETITE

FIGURE 1-2   **Pear-shape Body Type**

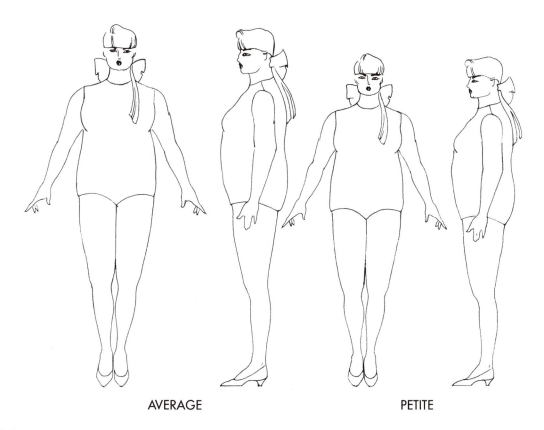

AVERAGE   PETITE

FIGURE 1-3   **Barrel-shape Body Type**

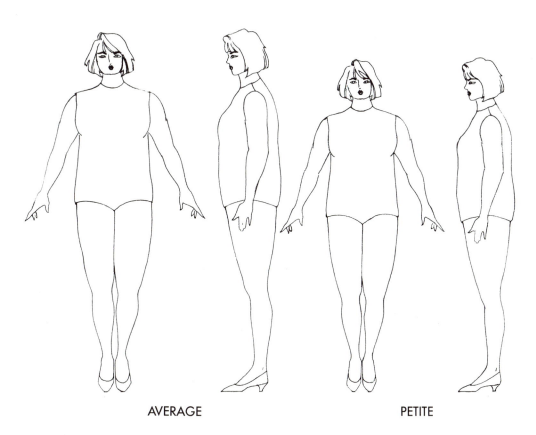

AVERAGE   PETITE

FIGURE 1-4   **Box-shape Body Type**

support a hunch, will ask the opinion of a favorite buyer who is consistently successful in anticipating customer reaction. They are all part of a team entrusted with decision-making on what styles stay in the line.

The merchandising team should direct their attention to the following as they examine each style:

- If the fabric is expensive, but beautiful and timely, will it be possible to keep labor and trimming costs to a minimum to stay within the price line? Fabric and silhouette will become the emphasis for this style.

- Detail in one area of the design may require simplicity in another area to keep labor costs at a minimum or even.

- Extravagant trimming means labor costs must be cut and less expensive fabric used.

- A style may look magnificent on a model but because of costly and complex construction becomes too expensive to produce.

- Styles may look terrific on a model but not on a hanger and may not arouse a buyer's or customer's interest. Unless this problem can be solved, the style should be discarded. The rule of thumb: the chances for success are greater if the garment looks well on the hanger.

- Will the style, in production, remain a close duplication of the original sample?

Each season the responsibility to minimize risk rests upon the opinions of the manufacturer's merchandising team. The success of the business depends on a collection that sells and reorders well. A garment must compete in an established marketplace and this team has to be constantly aware of how their styles fit into the price structure of the stores and departments selling their apparel. To keep the same retail customer, the line should display a consistent price structure and image.

Costing a Garment

A manufacturer will always cost a garment before establishing the wholesale price. It is necessary to work out the cost balance in advance of showing the line to buyers to prevent a need to lower costs through substitutions in stock shipped to the stores. Ideally, stock shipped to retailers should duplicate the original sample as close as possible. Stock that is watered down from the original sample shown to the buyer leaves them dissatisfied while a close duplication strengthens their trust in the manufacturer.

In the garment industry, the pricing of a garment must take into consideration:

- **Labor** Operating, finishing and pressing costs plus a percentage for cost of living (adjusted to reflect the prevailing cost of living).

- **Floor** A flat figure to cover the costs of draping, examining and cleaning. The amount is determined by the wholesale price of a garment.

- **Cutting** Sometimes done at a contractor, sometimes at the manufacturer. It is considered part of the labor costs. The manufacturer sets a minimum cut figure—the smallest amount the firm will cut. If the number of orders for a style is less than the minimum cut figure, the style is dropped from the line.

- **Contractor** When all the labor costs have been totaled, the contractor charges from thirty to forty percent (depending on the price point of the firm) for their overhead and profit.

- **Fringe Benefits** An additional percentage is added to the total labor costs to cover employee fringe benefits.

- **Fabric** The approximate price of the total yardage used to make the garment.

- **Trimming** The price of whatever else is needed to finish the garment.

fall 1988

Portraits of Fall

Justin Allen Xtra features spectacular variety, vitality and romance in dressing for the many moods of Fall. First there is **Mixed Media**, mixing and matching patterns including plaids, snowflakes and florals – the variety of pattern mixing is endless. And there's **Patches**, the perfect complement to Mixed Media. Then on to **A Touch of Class**, designs in fleece with satin trims, adding sweet luxury to the season. And to top it off, we have **Pigment-Dyed** bottoms for that in-fashion washed-out look.

A

Contact: Paul Schneiderman • 1350 Broadway • New York 10018 • Suite 400 • 212.239.1530

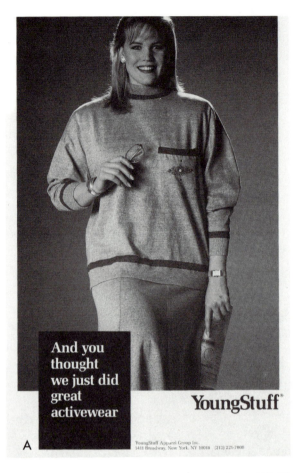

And you thought we just did great activewear

YoungStuff®

A

YoungStuff Apparel Group Inc.
1411 Broadway, New York, NY 10018   (212) 221-7800

RESSLER ENTERPRISES

presents

Evan-Picone Plus Coats

Sizes 14+ to 24+

Showing Fall '88

by appointment
(212) 239-7272

499 Seventh Avenue • New York City, New York 10018
2nd Floor, North Tower

C

The Re Kollection *Ltd*

'Round The Clock Dressing

Sizes 14-24

B

A

FIGURE 2-1   Develop an identity. Which resource will you specialize in for the plus-size?
A. Career and active sportswear?
B. Round-the-clock dressing for contemporary clothes?
C. Coats?
D. Career sportswear for the young professional?
E. The at-home, social minded plus-size?
F. At-home loungewear?
G. Round-the-clock dressing for classic clothes?

12

E

D

G

THE ULTIMATE FOR EASY LIVING...

Loungewear at it's best and
most attractive for the
Queen-size image!

For Orders Please Call Collect· 1-305-978-3006 or 978-3101

Michael/Drew, Inc.
Manufacturers Ladies Leisurewear & Loungewear
Whispering Lakes/2101 N.W. 33rd St., Suite A-1200/Pompano Beach, Florida 33069

F

Chez

CALIFORNIA, INC.

*Our dresses are for the woman
who wants to look and feel
her best.
We specialize in casual,
career, day through dinner and
after five dressing.*

Executive Office:
744 East 14th Place
Los Angeles, CA 90021
(213) 747-4477

Corporate Office:
1411 Broadway #1225
New York, NY 10018
(212) 840-6510

13

FIGURE 2-2   **Differentiate and cost-position against competing offerings.**

- **Manufacturer's Profit**   The garment manufacturer adds from forty to fifty percent of the total amount of all the above to cover overhead (the total cost of running a business), and profit. The profit usually comes to ten percent of the manufacturer's total costs of producing the garment (the wholesale price).

This breakdown determines the wholesale price of a garment—the retail price is usually double the wholesale price.

Marketing Knowhow . . . A Necessity

Manufacturers are confident that plus-size customers want fashion—pretty and elegant styles in fashionable colors and innovative fabrics—and are willing to pay the price for clothes that fit. These companies are willing to take a risk, but find that department store buyers are reluctant to do the same. It becomes necessary for the manufacturer to hang in there until the customer becomes aware of them.

Manufacturers must do their homework and know they have the right product that will create profitable sales and ensure their survival. Manufacturers need to get together with retailers who are on the same wavelength. Partnerships should be formed between the "create-and-market" and those on the "buy-and-sell" side of special sizes. Manufacturers have the duty to serve as tutors to retailers, helping with merchandising, presentation, the layout needs of a department or the training of sales personnel. It is the obligation of the partners to share information of value that will help to understand who their plus-size customer really is beyond what the demographics tell them. Manufacturers must ultimately depend on the retailers to carry the message about their product to consumers in a way they would want to do it themselves. Manufacturers need to become expert marketers.

Marketing is defined as, "the aggregate of functions involved in transferring title and in moving goods from producer to consumer, including among others buying, selling, storing, transporting, standardizing, financing, risk-bearing, and supplying market information." Marketing within the context of the large-size manufacturing industry is a strategic function that includes the following activities. The first three have been discussed, but their importance cannot be overemphasized:

1. Identify the customer and target customer market.

2. Identify the needs and wants of your market and the capabilities to respond to them.

3. Develop apparel to most efficiently satisfy your target market and return optimum profit. This demands that your product be differentiated and cost-positioned against competing offerings.

4. Product positioning:
   - Development of a total image—packaging, labeling, brand name, and the personality definition that describes and relates the becoming garment styles directly to its plus-size target market while at the same time differentiating it from competition.

   - Communications strategy—advertising, sales promotion and publicity such as televised fashion shows and commercials, and in-store fashion shows that will build awareness and preference for your garments.

   - Sales strategy—means by which the garments will be sold to the target market (fashion shows at stores).

   - Distribution strategy—to convey the styles to the plus-size targets through retail (an example is Bullock's advertising the manufacturer's styles of Givenchy En Plus), direct marketing when the manufacturer advertises through media, magazines, newspapers, etc., listing where styles can be found.

   - Development of a price for the garment relative to the dollar value the buyer is willing to spend in order to buy and that will still retain the manufacturer's desired profit and better than competing garments.

Developing marketing expertise and sophistication will help raise public consciousness of and interest in your plus-size fashions. You need to discover that intangible something that will make your merchandise different from that of your competitor's and that will stand out in a store. Provide the stores with in-store presentations of merchandising boards showing color stories to create multiple sales. A strong color theme, attractively displayed and carried out in many fabrications will make it easy to attract your customer and assist her in coordinating a wardrobe.

The plus-size customer is a loyal customer and will return to the store and the clothes from the manufacturer that give her the fashion she looks for and fits her body type. Stores on the other hand should be encouraged to provide large-size mannequins, large-size dressing rooms, large-size hangers and clothing positioned

Bullock's WOMAN

Opens Saturday September 19

It's our separate and complete store just for the fuller figure

You'll find us on the first level in the Woodland Hills Promenade Mall

ALL THE STYLE YOU LOVE

The larger-sized woman has a world of fashion options. We have a truly terrific and unique collection of clothes for every aspect of your life, from career to casual to social. You'll also enjoy a superb selection of intimate apparel and exciting accessories. At last, everything you've been looking for is here.

SHOPPING IS SO CONVENIENT

All the style and service you love about Bullock's is available to you at Bullock's Woman. The same fashion expertise. Now focused just on your needs. And you may use your Bullock's charge card for all your purchases. We also accept VISA, MasterCard and The American Express Card.

DESIGNING JUST FOR YOU

The list of names is impressive. Now they design especially for the fuller figure woman. Givenchy En Plus, Evan-Picone, Bettina Leathers, Susan Sandhaus, I.B. Diffusion, ABS, Villager, Chez, Beverly Hills Polo Club, Bonnie Boerer, Outlander, Gregge Sport, Fads, Judith Ann, Gemini II, WR II, Diane Von Furstenberg, Samuel Scott, Nightworks and more.

ROSES & MUSIC & MAKEOVERS

Visit our store on Saturday, opening day, and we'll greet you with a long-stemmed rose. Enjoy beautiful chamber music while you shop. And ask for a complimentary makeover courtesy of the CHANÉL artists.

A SPECIAL FASHION SHOW

We've planned a spectacular fashion show Saturday at 1:30 in the Center Court. It will be hosted by Paula Gallemore who is a noted expert on fuller figure fashions.

MEET THE FASHION EXPERTS

Enjoy a conversation with the people who create the clothes you want to wear. On hand opening day will be: Laura Chambers from Beverly Hills Polo Club; Susan Sandhaus, designer for Susan Sandhaus; Helen Lipton from I.B. Diffusion; and Alfredo Lopez, designer of Alfredo.

THE LOOKS FEATURED

Our featured spectacular, beaded silk chemise and co black with silver sequins, 1x, 2x, 3x, by Judith Ann, Susan Sandhaus ensemble i wool, 1x, 2x, 3x. Cardigan, Tank, 98.00. Pants, 114. Givenchy En Plus career dres copper wool. Jacket, 265. Pant, 130.00. Black window polyester blouse, 165.00

THINK BIG

FIGURE 2-3   Manufacturers must depend on retailers to carry the message about their product to consumers.

attractively on large-size racks. These amenities show the customer they have made a commitment to service her.

When you assemble and back a collection you believe in, based on a sound knowledge of the look your customer is after, and when the retailer presents your merchandise so as to catch a customer's eye, you will do well in the marketplace. Manufacturers and retailers working together in such a partnership will find rewards that will benefit them both.

FIGURE 2-4   TOP LEFT/RIGHT: Nancy Radmin of "The Forgotten Woman" says her customer base is not limited by income or age, but rather by taste level. Pull-out racks at "The Forgotten Woman" help with additional sales. LEFT: The bar is a perfect respite from the hectic pace of shopping. Also, convenient seating makes shopping a pleasure for everyone. BELOW: Jeanne Rafal's customer is 24–45 years old and is definitely a working woman who is upward mobile with an annual income from $20,000–$100,000, and with a family.

FIGURE 2-5 TOP LEFT: Hubert Givenchy fitting one of his designs on his fit model. Fit, quality and value are the elements of success for his Givenchy En Plus Collection. TOP RIGHT: Runway fashion shows are an important selling tool for retailers. RIGHT: The plus-size woman caught in a variety of poses and attitudes—fun and funky, dramatically alluring and professional.

3 A Blueprint for Figure Flattering Garments

The influence of the top designers is felt throughout the "slim" world but not in the big world. Style trends have rarely been designed exclusively for the large woman. However, the same elements and principles of design apply to both the slim and the big world.

In order to design a line of fashionable clothes for the plus-size customer, your first step should be to understand the large body. Learn how to emphasize the good body facts and de-emphasize the bad. Think in terms of the total picture each body type presents. Color, line, silhouette, fabric and garment details must all balance with the size and shape of the body. You must instinctively know when your design creates the balance and harmony that will make big women look terrific. You can prove to the world that your large-size customers can look as good as anyone if they have the same kind of clothes that their slim sisters have always had access to. To embrace the influences of the top designers, decisions must be made that are appropriate to the needs of the fuller figure while still leaning in the direction of the most current looks and forecasts.

Elements & Principles of Design

Master the elements and principles of design that play a crucial role in the total appearance of your customer. The elements of design are *line, value, texture and pattern*, and *color*. The principles of design are *proportion, balance, rhythm, emphasis* and *unity*. When the elements of design are blended in combinations as the principles of design dictate, they should create pleasing effects on the human figure. As a designer for the plus-size woman, you will want to select those combinations that will make the full figure appear more slender; combinations that are flattering, comfortable to wear and suitable to your plus-size customer's lifestyle.

Line—To Create Flattering Illusions

Line, as applied to fashion design, refers to the contour or outline of a garment as well as the

FIGURE 3-1

space within the outline. Style lines divide the space within a garment. When the eye comes in contact with a line it inadvertently follows it and gives emphasis to that point. Lines placed advantageously will lead the eye to the area of a garment to be emphasized and effectively draw it away and de-emphasize the problem areas.

The Silhouette Line

The silhouette line is created by the outline of the garment—the cut and the outer shape. At first glance, the size and shape of the garment is recognized by its silhouette line. The eye then focuses on the other design elements included in the garment and receives a total impression. The silhouette because it is the dominant optical line, dictates many of the other design elements included in the design.

There should be a direct relationship between the silhouette line and the body lines. The shape of the silhouette should complement the shape of the body. The silhouette line should appear as a natural extension of the body lines and create a beautiful balance. Exaggeration is often used to create a special effect or balance to enhance the full figure. The overall silhouette is dictated by prevailing fashion.

The Style Line

Style lines create visual illusions such as height to make a figure seem taller or shorter, and width to make a figure seem thinner or heavier. The illusion a line conveys is stronger when thickened and contrasted to the rest of the garment. Straight (horizontal and vertical), diagonal and curved lines are all used in garment design to visually deceive the eye.

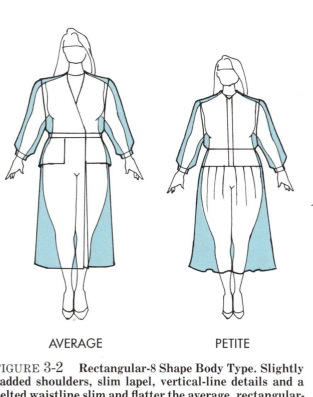

AVERAGE   PETITE

FIGURE 3-2   **Rectangular-8 Shape Body Type.** Slightly padded shoulders, slim lapel, vertical-line details and a belted waistline slim and flatter the average, rectangular-8 body type. This body type is well-proportioned and appears to benefit from most styles. This classic shirtdress has a slim silhouette, slightly padded shoulders and a pointed collar. Vertical line in the hidden opening carries the eye upward to elongate the body and balance the petite rectangular-8 shape.

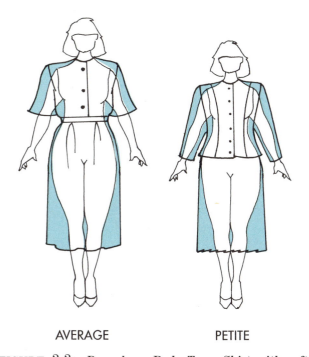

AVERAGE   PETITE

FIGURE 3-3   **Pear-shape Body Type.** Skirt with soft unpressed pleats and belt detail move the eye high and away from large hips to the tailored patch pockets of the bodice, and also appears to broaden the chest. The extended padded shoulders are the extra equalizer to create body balance for the petite pear shape. Shoulder pads and vertical lines of the jacket, which stop just above the widest part of the body, will keep the eye up and will elongate and balance pear-shape figures.

AVERAGE

PETITE

AVERAGE

PETITE

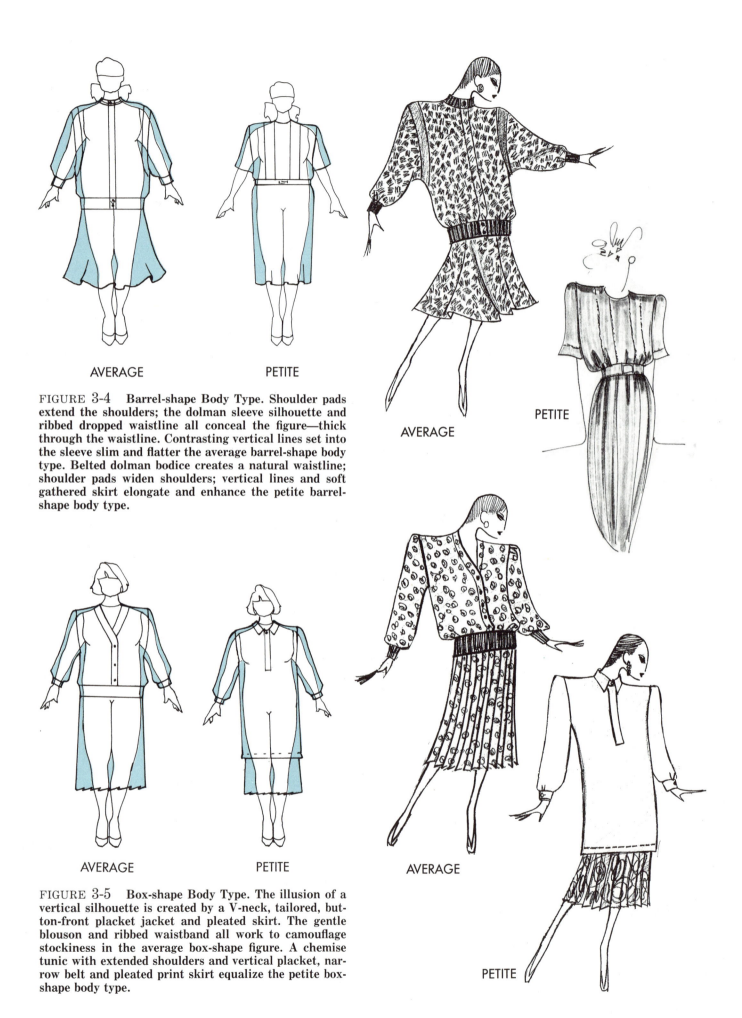

AVERAGE

PETITE

AVERAGE

PETITE

FIGURE 3-4 **Barrel-shape Body Type. Shoulder pads extend the shoulders; the dolman sleeve silhouette and ribbed dropped waistline all conceal the figure—thick through the waistline. Contrasting vertical lines set into the sleeve slim and flatter the average barrel-shape body type. Belted dolman bodice creates a natural waistline; shoulder pads widen shoulders; vertical lines and soft gathered skirt elongate and enhance the petite barrel-shape body type.**

AVERAGE

PETITE

AVERAGE

PETITE

FIGURE 3-5 **Box-shape Body Type. The illusion of a vertical silhouette is created by a V-neck, tailored, button-front placket jacket and pleated skirt. The gentle blouson and ribbed waistband all work to camouflage stockiness in the average box-shape figure. A chemise tunic with extended shoulders and vertical placket, narrow belt and pleated print skirt equalize the petite box-shape body type.**

24

Straight vertical lines create length and suggest dignity and strength. Vertical illusions keep the eye moving upward for a taller and thinner look. Silhouettes which emphasize vertical lines add height to the figure. A straight vertical line gives the illusion of a longer and sleeker effect and divides the figure making it seem thinner. Vertical lines are appropriate for all body types.

Horizontal lines suggest a lack of movement, a pause. The horizontal line stops the eye from moving upward and the appearance of height is diminished. Seams or fashion details horizontally placed will create the illusion of width. Horizontal illusions make narrow shoulders appear broader. Horizontal lines that carry the eyes across the top part of the body add a bit of visual width creating the illusion of a narrower hipline. Horizontal illusions should be used for body types to achieve pleasing proportions.

Diagonal lines suggest movement. They are artful and sophisticated attracting attention to one detail. Diagonal lines when combined with vertical lines carry the eye upward and have a slenderizing effect making the figure seem taller (**Figure 3-8**). Diagonal lines will slim the figure if the angle is not too abrupt. Diagonal lines in a garment tend to slenderize the whole more than abrupt vertical lines (**Figure 3-9**). A diagonal line usually creates an asymmetrical design.

Curved lines should be strong and rhythmic not weak and fussy. Curved lines lend youth and roundness to a figure. A gentle curve is feminine and passive. The more extreme a curved line becomes the longer it takes to view the contour and so it will seem fussy or unnecessary. Curved seam details that continue downward to the hemline give the illusion of a smooth figure. Curved lines may be used to add figure flattering fashion details and are effective for all body types.

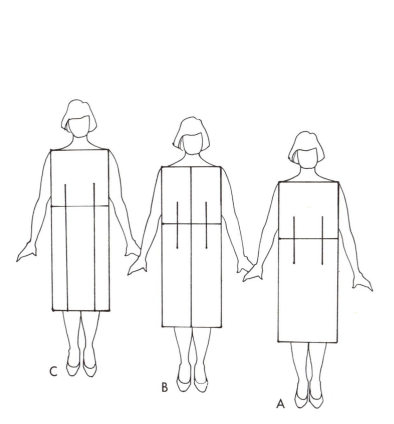

FIGURE 3-6 **Short vertical lines interrupted with a horizontal line in A give the widest illusion. The eye is carried across the whole figure to create the illusion of width. The figure appears thinner in B and C, because the vertical lines are interrupted less often.**

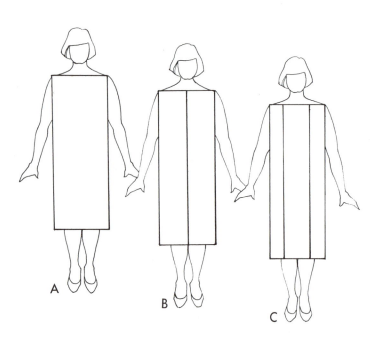

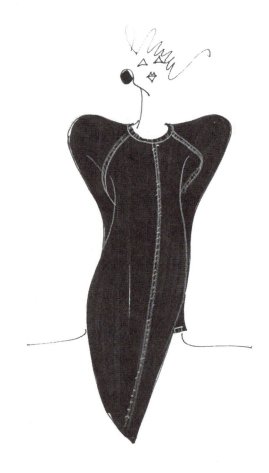

FIGURE 3-7   Vertical lines in B and C draw the eye upward and make the figure appear taller and slimmer than A. The additional vertical line in C divides the body into a smaller whole to create the illusion of a slimmer as well as a taller figure.

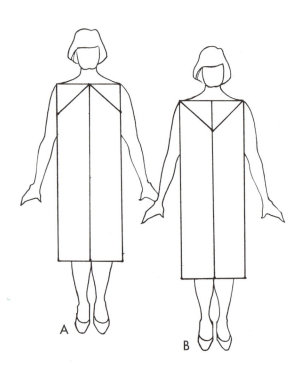

FIGURE 3-8   The upward movement of the diagonal lines in A provide the illusion of height. The horizontal line across the top in B stops the eye from moving upward and reduces the illusion of height.

FIGURE 3-9   Which figure in this group looks the widest? The short vertical lines in C do not lead the eye over the whole to achieve the slimmest result. On the other hand, the diagonal lines in A slenderize the whole more than short vertical lines.

FIGURE 3-9

FIGURE 3-10   Horizontal lines with vertical and diagonal line combinations. The horizontal line in B directs the eye across the body emphasizing its width at that part.

FIGURE 3-10

FIGURE 3-11   The style lines in these garments are excellent examples of the use of strong and rhythmic curves for the plus-size.

FIGURE 3-11

Value—Its Optical Illusions

The manner in which a space is divided into areas by lines influences the appearance of a garment. Even horizontal divisions of space shorten and widen the visual length of a garment. Uneven horizontal divisions of space shorten and widen *and* lengthen and thin the visual length of a garment. The shapes which result from the use of these lines must vary in size and contour and may be emphasized by the use of dark and light (value).

Webster defines value as "that property of color by which it is distinguished as light or dark, . . . the relation of one part or detail to another with respect to lightness or darkness." The contrast between light and dark is used frequently to conceal figure problems. The eye travels to light areas first. Light areas stand out making them seem larger than they are especially when contrasted with dark areas. It is more pleasing to have unequal areas of dark and light rather than equal areas.

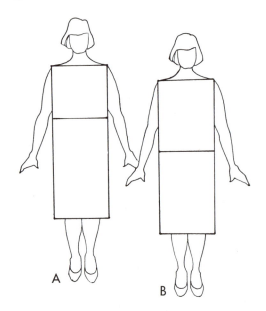

FIGURE 3-12 **Evenly divided spaces emphasize the squareness of a shape. Uneven horizontal divisions make the whole appear thinner.**

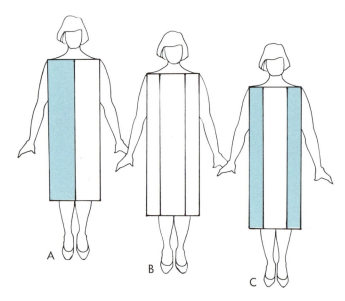

FIGURE 3-13 **A appears slimmer than B. The eye sees only half the figure as the dark side is less obvious. Light areas stand out making them seem larger, particularly when contrasted with dark areas as in C. The dark panels recede.**

FIGURE 3-14 **Light areas at V-neckline will focus attention to the face and make the figure appear taller. The vertical style lines slim the silhouette as well.**

FIGURE 3-15 **When the darker value is used below the waist, the hips appear smaller. The lighter bodice will make the bust seem larger.**

Texture—As It Affects Light and Dark

The textures and patterns of fabrics used in clothing design contribute to the dark and light appearance of the garment. Texture refers to the surface quality of fabric—its appearance. Texture is what gives character to a fabric and also refers to the hand, the way the fabric feels and drapes—soft and crisp, stiff or fluid, smooth or rough, dull or shiny.

Shiny textures have sharp highlights and dark shadows. They increase size and reveal the silhouette. Shiny textures (satin, silk, polished cotton, etc.) as well as pile fabrics (velvet, velour, corduroy, terrycloth, chenille, etc.) reflect a great deal of light creating an optical illusion that makes the garment and figure appear larger. On the other hand, fabrics with flat textures and dull surfaces absorb light and minimize size.

Bulky or rough-textured fabrics and stiff or crisp fabrics tend to increase size and add pounds to the ample figure. Although they increase size, they also conceal the silhouette and some body faults. Stiff or crisp fabrics are best for a design with a simple silhouette line with vertical emphasis that uses minimum fabric.

Prints add another dimension to fabric. The selection is unlimited along with the potential for creating a fashionable garment. Patterns work best when in scale with the size of the body and when analyzed for their dark and light value. Busy patterns draw attention. Directional patterns emphasize the figure because the eye follows the direction in which they flow. Vertical patterns may lead the eye across the figure or up and down in a quick uninterrupted glance to make the figure seem broader or more slender. Medium-size patterns with close color contrasts are the most becoming to all body types. Light and bright colors, sharp contrasts and large motifs will increase size while darker, muted, overall patterns will decrease size.

Texture and pattern of fabrics are capable of emphasizing or de-emphasizing the ample figure. Use both eye-deceiving capabilities to create the best looking clothes for the ample size customer.

FIGURE 3-16 Light crisp fabrics tend to increase size, but when used with dark vertical and horizontal lines they present a vertical emphasis to the torso and add width to the shoulders, concealing the faults of a pear-shape body type.

FIGURE 3-17 Prints with flat textures and dull surfaces absorb light and minimize size.

FIGURE 3-18 **Dark crisp fabrics with light vertical lines minimize size and have a vertical emphasis. Ideal for the barrel-shape body type.**

Color

Color is that aspect of fashion that holds everything together, the element of design that makes clothes exciting and glamorous. Color is an integral part of the fashion scene and an indispensable means for achieving illusions that will flatter all figure types. There are twelve basic colors beginning with *Red, Blue* and *Yellow*—the three pure *primary colors*. These are blended in equal amounts and form three more colors called *secondary colors—Orange, Green* and *Purple*. When equal amounts of primary and secondary colors are blended six more colors are created—*Yellow-Orange, Red-Orange, Red-Violet, Yellow-Green, Blue-Green,* and *Blue-Violet*—called *tertiary colors*. These twelve basic colors can be blended together in different quantities and combinations to form endless amounts of other colors.

Since not all colors are created equal, evaluate color by its *value*—that property of color which is distinguished by lightness or darkness—and *shade*—its brilliance or luminosity and intensity, the degree of brightness or dullness. The lighter colors are colors to which white has been added (red with white added equals pink, a lighter shade of red). The darker colors are colors to which black has been added (red with black added equals maroon, a darker shade of red). Lighter shades because of the white added reflect light and can make the large-size customer look a few sizes larger. The darker shades because black is added, absorb light, making the large-size customer appear smaller. Remember light colors increase size and dark colors diminish size. A garment in one long line of color or tones of that color will advance the illusion of height and in a dark color will achieve a slenderizing effect as well.

Value / Shade / Intensity

The properties of color—*value*, *shade* and *intensity*—are the how to's for putting colors together successfully. Colors of the same intensity work well together. Bright colors with dull colors do not. Dusty pink (light and dull) and maroon (dark and dull) is a good combination. Hot pink (light and intense) and maroon (dark and dull) is not. Hot pink and fuchsia work well together because they both have the same intensity. Bright colors clamor for attention, increase the size of the figure and reveal the silhouette. Dull colors on the other hand will decrease size and conceal the silhouette. Bright colors should be used in small areas for flattering results. Light colors are flattering around the face. The eye seeks out light colors when they contrast with dark colors. Let's take your customer with a large bust and slender hips (the barrel-shape body type). You can equalize her figure with light-colored pants and a dark top. The slenderizing mystic of color is contrast and contrasting color can be a lot more subtle than a dark top and light pants combinatioin. Contrasting color will break up horizontal lines and create vertical illusions.

Warm colors (red, orange, yellow) are advancing colors and therefore carry the illusion of weight. They are difficult to wear. A belt in a warm color directs the eye to that area immediately maximizing size. Enclosing a shape with a dark outline in a contrasting color will emphasize that area of the body. Texture or pattern shapes of advancing colors against a plain background will magnify the shape.

Cool colors (blue, green, violet) are receding colors and tend to minimize the size of the figure. Receding colors without bold outlines create flattering effects. Plain unbroken shapes tend to recede and can be emphasized with an area of texture or detail to direct the eye to it. An area filled with pattern will seem larger than a plain area. You can combine a bold treatment with a neutral or flattering color to create an equalizing effect for your customer with a small bust and large hips (the pear-shape body type). An example would be a bright bold pattern top with dark pants. The focus of attention will be on the bust and bodice and will lead the eye to the face, especially if the neckline is V-shaped.

FIGURE 3-19 TOP: Light colors clamor for attention and increase size. Dull or dark colors do not. Equalize the pear-shape body type with a light top and dark pants. RIGHT: Contrast can be the slenderizing mystic of color. Contrasting colors will break up horizontal lines and create vertical illusions.

We have discussed the elements of design; line, value, texture and pattern and color, and have examined how each relates to the physical characteristics of the large-size body types. You have come to understand the limitations of the ample figure. You can turn these limitations into assets providing the elements of design are combined as dictated by the principles of design. An examination of the principles of design is now in order.

Principles of Design

A well-designed garment is one that is harmonious in line and value (dark and light), includes the right pattern, the correct amount of texture and color relationships. These elements may be manipulated in various ways according to the principles of design (proportion, balance, harmony, rhythm and emphasis). Line, value, texture and pattern, and color are grouped so as to create good proportion, balance and harmony. These must exist in each garment. Rhythm must be embodied in the lines used and emphasis must be placed so that the center of interest is significant. The elements of design, therefore, must be used so as to produce a unified and harmoniously organized whole which is pleasing to the eye and at the same time enhances the attractiveness of your plus-size customer.

Proportion

By definition proportion is the "number, size, or amount of a thing or group" or "to put (one thing) in a right relation (to another)" or "in proportion (to) in proper or pleasing relation; in balance or harmony (with)." Proportion, the relationship of the sizes of the different parts and divisions of a garment and the bulk of a garment as it relates to the size of your large-size customer's body is the consideration here.

Ancient Greek costumes were the ideal of good proportion. The Greeks carried the esthetic into every phase of life. Their costumes attained the very height of perfection in symmetry, proportion, and line. (The simplest effect in drapery was the result of much care and speculation.) Fabrics were woven by the women of the house, of wool and flax, dyed many colors, though white was also used. The flowing garment in these fabrics extended from neck to ankles and was girdled at the natural waistline. The garment was broken into two parts, one of which was less than half of the whole amount while the other was more than half. This indicates that in order to have a pleasing effect, the division of a garment must fall either somewhere between one-third

FIGURE 3-20

and one-half or one-half and two-thirds of an area. Equal divisions should be avoided because they are monotonous, having no variety. The following are optical illusions that the proportion of a garment and its parts convey to the viewer.

- The eye automatically compares the smaller portion of a garment with the larger portion, making a garment divided unequally seem longer.

- Width above and/or below an area makes the area seem smaller.

- Similar horizontal divisions of space shorten and widen the visual length of a garment.

The illustrations in **Figure 20** demonstrate the principles of proportion. As a designer you will constantly experiment with subtle variations in proportion—where to place the style line, the length of the skirt, the size and placement of details—until the combined elements achieve the desired effect. Remember seamlines and hem edges form the vertical and horizontal lines that divide sections of a garment. These lines can make your customer look taller and slimmer, or shorter and broader. Achieving good proportion in your designs takes time and experience.

FIGURE 3-20

Balance

When the design of a garment has proper balance it is restful to the eye. There are two methods to achieve balance. The *equal* or *symmetrical* balance is the most widely used and occurs when the arrangement of the elements of design on a garment are the same on each side of the center of the body. The right and left front of the garment are the same. A dress with a center front seam and details of equal size placed on each side of the center front is an example of equal balance.

The other type of balance is called *unequal* or *asymmetrical*. It is the balance between elements of unequal size or weight. Unequal or asymmetrical balance is more intricate and far more interesting when properly manipulated. Designing an asymmetrical garment requires more thought, observation and experimentation. If a detail is placed on one hip, something must be placed on the other side of the garment to balance that detail, and prevent the garment from looking one sided. Many of the garments of the Restoration Period were designed using unequal balance.

We have discussed balance and proportion in order to achieve good design. It is necessary and most important that the balance and proportion in a garment should be in balance and harmony with the body size and shape. The focal point of a garment is used for balance. You need to bring one part of the body, top or bottom, into balance. You need to utilize the elements of design to make each body type look evenly formed, top and bottom. It is very important to create a balanced look for your plus-size customer.

Harmony

A feeling of harmony will result when there is good proportion and proper balance in the design of a garment. Harmony will exist when all elements of design work together to produce a successful visual effect. The following will help you to understand and achieve harmony for your design.

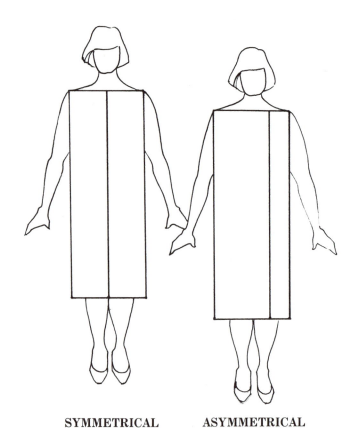

SYMMETRICAL   **ASYMMETRICAL**

FIGURE 3-21

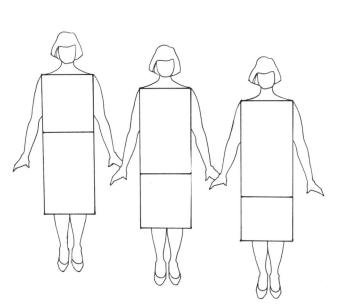

FIGURE 3-22   **The illusion of height is increased even when the unequal divisions are reversed and the emphasis is placed on the hips.**

FIGURE 3-23   The greater the difference between the size of the bodice and the skirt the taller the figure will look.

FIGURE 3-22

- All style lines should be consistent on all areas of the garment.

- All areas of the garment should reflect the same shapes.

- The length of sleeves should relate to the horizontal lines of the garment. Sleeve lengths should be planned and aligned with horizontal details.

- All stripes and plaids should match, especially on sleeves that hang parallel to the garment.

- All seamlines and details on the sleeve should align with similar lines and details on the garment.

- Style lines should have compatible angles on all areas of the garment and must complement each other.

To master the principle of harmony analyze garments that are pleasing to you. Train your eye to recognize the successful use of harmony in garments. Research and study the master designers.

FIGURE 3-24 **Rhythm.**

Rhythm

Rhythm is the recurrent use of lines or shapes to create patterns. Equal rhythm is the repetition of the same space. In graduated rhythm the size and space increases or decreases as it is repeated. Unequal rhythm is the unequal use of space. Unequal or graduated rhythm is usually the more desirable method for breaking up horizontal space.

Lines should lead rhythmically toward any feature that you wish to emphasize and away from any feature you do not want to call attention to. Because curved lines are more compatible to the shape of the body a series of curves will express rhythm better than a series of angles or geometric lines. Careful experimentation is necessary to design a garment that has pleasing rhythm to flatter the plus-size customer.

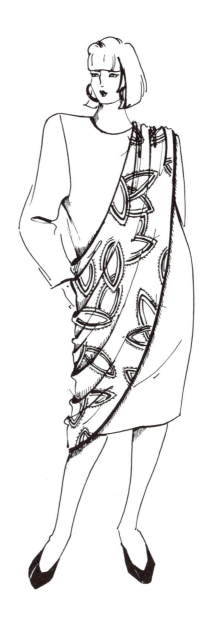

FIGURE 3-25   **Emphasis.**

FIGURE 3-26   **Emphasis.**

Emphasis

Line has the power to lead the eye and to give emphasis to that point. As soon as the eye comes in contact with a line, it naturally and unconsciously follows the line. Emphasis creates a center of interest when the eye is drawn to a specific area of the garment. As a designer, use the principle of emphasis to direct the eye to what you wish to emphasize. The ideal design has a chief center of interest with perhaps a subordinate interest or two elsewhere on the garment.

Contrasting colors and trims are also used to achieve emphasis. Dark areas on a light-colored garment and white or light areas on a dark-col-

ored background emphasize the area of the body where they are placed.

There is no need to compromise fashion for the plus-size customer. Designs will be a work of *good taste* if unity is observed. When every part and every detail contribute to oneness, a harmonious whole is achieved. The principles of design—*proportion, balance, harmony, rhythm* and *emphasis*—are guides to develop the relation of the parts of a garment to the whole. Interest is maintained when these principles are used properly with the elements of design—*line, value, texture and pattern,* and *color.*

4 Designing a Line for the Plus-Size Customer

The design process usually begins at least eighteen months or so before the garments are seen at the retail level. Color and fabric specialists worldwide predict the colors and fabrications for the new fashion season. Color choices follow a loosely defined cycle, strongly influenced by the successes and failures of recent seasons. The color specialists gather and computerize such information, consulting fabric and fashion companies to assimilate a consensus of opinion. The colors created are then subject to the industry's individual tastes. The new season's colors and fabrications are made available to designers before they begin their new collections. Designers begin work on their new line six to eight months before the shipping date. The first showing of the new line usually takes place three months before the shipping date.

Fashion means change and change is the new becoming old and old ideas becoming new again. In pursuit of the new most designers watch for the earliest hints of coming trends. They scrutinize new styles created by the world's leading

FIGURE 4-1 **Designer Hubert Givenchy working on his collection for Givenchy En Plus.**

39

FIGURE 4-2   Season's colors and fabrications are made available to designers before they begin their collections. Here you see the various elements included in a forecasting kit from "The Color Box."

fashion designers, introduced each year in Milan, New York, Paris and elsewhere. These collections are filled with bright ideas that blend wonderful fabrications with new fashion silhouettes. They present a stock of fashion images from which each designer draws her/his inspiration. They are fashion pioneers.

Each year buyers, fashion editors and manufacturers swarm to these fashion capitals for an in-depth review of the colors, fabrics, prints and silhouettes favored. Following the shows, a surge of fashion predictions appear in fashion forecast publications. The forecasting services analyze, examine and illustrate all the key directions, shapes and details. Fashion designers look to forecasting publications as a base of reference to reinterpret the fashions in the latest colors, fabrics and shapes for their customer's lifestyle and their company's limitations. Published sources of fashion and consumer trends are basic to a designer's weekly reading (see **page 187** for a list of sources).

The continual search for something fresh is the designers greatest challenge. For many designers reading the trade paper, *Women's Wear Daily*, is a good way to keep up with what's happening in fashion. The more a designer reads, the more imaginative ideas will be. Ideas and concepts are drawn from all over the world, from the past and present. Designers will review fashions of the past and may be inspired to introduce them again—but with new appeal. Ideas come to mind based on feedback from the economy, cultural events and politics to what's being worn on the streets and what sold well the season before. Ideas brew when on vacation, here and abroad, listening to suggestions from stores, and what one hears from customers.

As the designer researches and evaluates the information gathered to meet the challenge of designing for individuals, he/she translates this information into the image the line will project far in advance of the actual selling season. The designer begins the design process with the right color choices, then shops the fabric market, and finally sketches the garment designs.

The Color Story

The first step in the design process is to select the colors for your collections, coordinating them into combinations that will color your customer beautiful. The correct use of color can help the eye see not so much a large woman, but a well-dressed one.

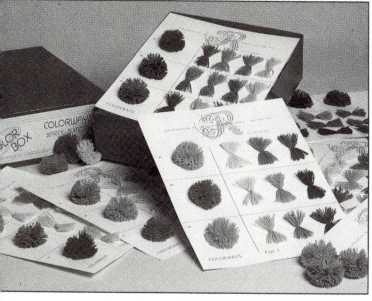

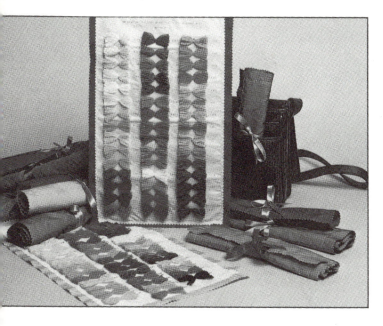

When shopping for clothing the customer's initial reaction is to color, which may be as visible as a few inches on a rack or display. This initial attraction determines whether she takes a closer look, touches and further examines the garment's allover pattern fabrication and silhouette. Color may be the deciding factor as to whether the garment will be tried on and bought. Color calls attention to itself. One is more apt to say "I'll examine the garment on the rack with the blue sleeve" rather than ". . . the garment with the long sleeve."

The plus-size customer, regardless of her body-type measurements, is aware of color and its ability to create optical illusions. This sophistication further increases the power of color as a selling tool. Designers must, therefore, pay the palette all due respect and attention. As discussed in the previous chapter, color consists of primary, secondary and tertiary colors, which in different quantities and combinations form unlimited colors. Evaluate colors when putting them together. Light colors reflect light and will increase size. Dark colors absorb light to dwindle size. Colors of the same intensity work well together; bright colors with dull colors do not. When you have mastered how to evaluate and understand color, you will be able to combine colors with pleasing and flattering results for your plus-size customers.

Color Creates Optical Illusions

Color can create the illusion of a longer, sleeker body. If properly used it can conceal body proportions and de-emphasize a figure flaw. When used in small prints, uneven plaids and stripes, it can create a slenderizing image. Harmonious and muted colors in prints convey a one-color illusion. Harmonizing vertical stripes in the right color will have a narrowing effect as will textured fabric with vertical ribs. Color should appear to flow from head to toe in smooth vertical lines to create the maximum illusion of height.

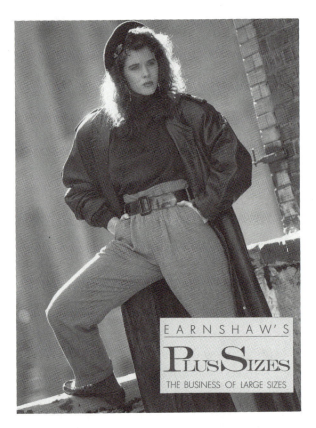

FIGURE 4-3 **Here is the cover for the press kit from** Plus Size **Magazine.**

A design in one shade of color allows for a variety of texture and adds interest without emphasizing size. Another use of color equally effective is to work with a spectrum of related shades that have basically the same tonality and are capable of blending into one another.

Contrasting Color

Contrasting colors are not created from the same basic color. They do not share one of the twelve basic (primary, secondary and tertiary) colors. Red and green are contrasting colors because red is a primary color and green is a secondary color created from blue and yellow. Green does not share the basic color red. On the other hand orange and purple are not contrasting colors. Orange (from red and yellow) and purple (from red and blue) share the basic color red. A word of caution on contrasting colors. Contrasting colors are usually strong colors and could create horizontal lines that direct attention to problem figure areas. Use contrasting colors to accent designs with a blouse, scarf or jewelry. Color

blocking in a design using contrasting colors with vertical lines such as a princess garment is slenderizing and can be a knockout statement.

Harmonizing Color

Harmonizing colors contain at least one similar primary color. You have to realize that not all harmonizing colors are created equal and therefore you should be careful about placing these colors together. The dye mix of fabric can make colors that should harmonize clash. Bluish-red and bluish-gray harmonize well because they have the same tone. Harmonizing colors are best for the large-size customer because they do not call attention to themselves as contrasting colors do.

Neutrals

Colors recognized as neutrals are black, white, gray, brown and beige. Neutrals are always in fashion and safe because they go with everything. Neutrals are particularly compatible to plus sizes. They are easier to put together than other colors (although be careful of the color tones some neutrals have), as they don't clamor for attention, in fact they recede into the background and diminish size. Neutrals can be used to create the illusion of a thinner, taller figure and are especially appropriate in one-color dressing. Neutrals are always elegant and tasteful.

Color as an Accent

A designer can create flattering illusions for plus-sizes by using color as an accent on some part of a garment, such as in a scarf, piping, trims, buttons, facings, appliqués, embroidery, collars and cuffs. Accent colors can de-emphasize a problem area of the body because they attract the eye and direct it to another part of the garment. A colorful collar or scarf can divert attention from large hips or a colorful trim on a skirt can draw the eye away from a large bust. Accent consists of contrasting, harmonizing or matching colors.

Matching colors will catch the eye provided the fabric texture of the accent is different than that of the garment. Color as an accent calls upon the imagination of a designer and must be used sparingly.

As you can see color has its own special prominence and impact and cannot be discussed under one heading. It is such an integral part of the fashion picture, especially as it relates to the plus-size customer, and is often underestimated.

Planning the Color Story

Colors should be seasonal, fashion right and offer enough diversity to encourage sales from the designer's line. Help with color direction is available through fiber companies and fabric converters. They publish color predictions at least eighteen months in advance of each season. In addition, there are color forecasting services designed specifically for the fashion industry. These forcasting services research and evaluate information gathered both here and abroad, and translate it into a color story geared to the American consumer. For example, The Color Box presents the current season's colors in a series of palettes and color combinations for inspiration with moveable yarn pompoms. Whatever forecast service you use, analyze the color predictions and determine the distinctive colors and color combinations best suited to the body types of your large-size customer.

The colors favored by designers are referred to as fashion colors and classic colors such as navy and gray are also called staple colors. The fashion colors are likely to change from season to season, while classic colors are available each season. Classic colors although available each season will look noticeably different from one season to the next. This creates some newness and additional excitement.

Your master colors (the color story theme) should consist of warm colors, cool colors, neutrals and darks to create a color language all their own, making the most pleasing optical illusions.

The selection of master colors for the plus-size customer should be made to include those colors that create one-color dressing, color accent, color contrast and color harmony for the most flattering results.

The number of colors to choose for the master color story varies. There can be a minimum of six to twelve or more colors depending on the size and image the line is to create.

Often the color statement can be inspired by the colors in a pattern of a favored printed fabric design. The designer will utilize these colors as the basis for their color story.

The color story shown (on our cover) inherits the color combinations in the wool plaid fabric and the color combinations of the printed design. The group of neutrals also attributes its inspiration to a printed fabric design. Neutrals traditionally stand together successfully with, for example, the added spark of patio peach as a tonal accent. Neutrals combine individually with other colors as well.

Selecting Fabric

Designers must function in many areas simultaneously. They need to consider color, fabric, line, proportion, and detail as well as the indefinable something that will give their line the distinctive aura the retailers have come to count on.

Textile designers and manufacturers play a key role in the design process interpreting fabric direction with enticing early forecasts of color and print. As they inspire the fashion designers, these fabrics often provide the first element in the total composition and are often the basis for deciding a color story.

Most designers agree that much of what is designed each season is predetermined. There are certain pieces that a designer must include in the line—jackets, skirts, blouses, T-shirts, pants and dresses depending on the reputation of the manufacturer. The line may include both dresses and sportswear or one or the other. If a piece did well the previous season, it will be repeated the following season. Usually each collection is half evolvement and half new ideas.

With knowing what the line or collection should consist of the designer begins the search for fabrics with colors approximating the tones in their color story. The search for fabrics for the next collection begins seriously as soon as a current collection is shown. Designers work at least six months ahead of the collection deadline, and it is likely you'll find them working with two seasons overlapping. This makes selecting fabrics difficult and challenging. Sometimes a beautiful fabric is selected and when it arrives a designer will ask, "Did I buy that?" and discard it because it no longer fits into the theme of the collection.

As you select fabric keep a clear-cut vision of how you want your large-size customer to look. Consider every aspect—fabric thickness, texture, color, size of the print or stripe. Select fabrics that lend themselves to the silhouette and to the optical illusions most alluring for the plus-size woman. Remember an impressive fashion statement begins with discriminately selected fabrics.

Structuring the Line

You've determined your color story and selected your fabrics, you are now faced with one of the most important functions—structuring the line. In high-priced firms, high fashion is important and the line may cover everything from sportswear to evening wear. The lower-priced firms are often more specialized in the category they will produce. In high-priced collections the sample garments are usually shown in groups separated by time of day. The showing may start with casual wear, go on to day wear, after-five and evening fashions. The manufacturer who specializes in daytime fashions on the other hand shows the sample garments grouped by fabrics, wool, silk, knit, novelties and so on.

Actually the designer structures the collection in the same groups it will be shown to buyers. Group lines are planned around fabrics and depending on the type of line and fabric, some garments are created specifically for each fabric. The groups must take into consideration a variety of customer likes and dislikes and offer customers a range of colors and styles becoming to each of the large-size body types. The groups should reflect a theme and include enough pieces to give buyers a choice. Lines planned by the group method should include:

- A group of styles made from one fabric or the same combination of fabrics. A story or styling theme evolves best by using one fabric for similar designs. This has the advantage of advertising money from fiber companies in exchange for the support of large fabric purchases and fashionable garments.

- A design or silhouette that did well last season can be repeated in a variety of fabrics at different price points.

- A group of dresses in soft fabrics in four or five different colors which are traditionally strong sellers.

- A group of novelty designs.

Each group should have variety of styles (different sleeve treatments, details, and necklines) but at the same time maintain the same theme. Each group should include styles appropriate to the body proportions of each of the full-figure body types as well. Single unit items—dresses, coats, suits that do not need to coordinate within a group—should adhere to a color story and silhouette theme. All groups should have the visual impact of being created by one person with a clear image and identity.

The designer should structure a collection so all styles maintain a constant visual image. You can easily lose perspective when designing a collection. A designer has to absorb what's new and know what to do with it, and at the same time not overdo a new trend. The ability to make a distinction of what's new and what's wearable and beautiful is necessary. A designer has to find a favorable balance between turning out a collection that is creative but acutely short on good wearable, saleable styles or go overboard in the other direction with nothing but bread-and-butter styles.

Fabric Boards

A fabric board consists of swatches of all the fabrics and trims a designer has chosen for each group with all the necessary style information recorded next to each swatch. As the line develops, it becomes the focal point of reference for fabric and styling decisions, because a fabric board shows at a glance what has been planned and purchased for each group. It presents a birdseye view of the progress that has been made in structuring the line.

Designer Workboards

A workboard is prepared at the start of each new season to keep an accurate record of all the styles a designer has created for each group including changes that are made to styles and the many designs that are discarded before the line is completed and sold. All the items that go into a group should be numbered. It is an excellent tool at merchandising meetings, as it shows at a glance all the items designed for a group.

Both reference tools, the fabric board and the designer workboard include all the necessary information to prepare a cost sheet for each item available in a collection. They should also contain information on all the details of a style, the source and price of buttons, trims, belts, etc. A description of each sample is given next to the sketch.

Creating the Design Sketches

All design samples begin with an idea by the designer. He/she communicates her/his idea through the use of a sketch. A designer may approach a design sketch in one of two ways. In the first approach a designer's idea may be full-blown (clear and precise in detail) and is sketched immediately or the idea evolves through a series of sketches. In the second approach the designer drapes the fabric on a mannequin (also called a dress form). There are designers who work mostly by sketching, others who work mostly by draping the fabric and still others who do both.

The designers who work by sketching may be so prolific with ideas, they turn out many sketches and find it hard to decide which ones to produce. For them the most difficult part of designing is editing their ideas and choosing the right fabric for the style.

The designers who create by draping the fabric begin as soon as the fabric arrives to study its weight and texture. The inspiration for the silhouette and style lines evolve as the fabric is draped. As progress is made the designer will solicit the opinions of her/his assistants. The idea takes shape in fabric and then a sketch is drawn. Fabrics dictate the designs. Coloring, textures and cuts simply define the mood, the shape and the fit.

There are very few women with perfect bodies regardless of their size. Different body types have individual figure problems, all an invitation for you to engage in the challenge—to design the best looking garment for them. The next chapter will illustrate how the influence of top designers can be translated to fashion for the plus-size woman.

FIGURE 4-4 **Designers should structure a collection to maintain a constant visual image.**

5 Interpreting Fashion for the Plus-Size Figure

The high fashion looks shown on the runways of New York, London, Paris and Milan, have been designated as the area of the *slim* fashion world. These high fashion looks eventually become diluted by the mass manufacturers and filter down to moderate-priced markets where they are accessible to most people.

Plus-size customers are being romanced with more fashion forward lines with the same stylish appeal as the offerings in smaller sizes than ever before. Large-size apparel in pretty, elegant styles, in fashionable colors and innovative prints is for all ages.

When the world's leading fashion designers show their new styles on the runways all over the world, keep in mind the plus-size customer. Remember the large woman wants clothes that not only minimize her size, but maximize her fashion impact. Therefore high fashion can be successfully interpreted for this customer. *Proportion* is the key word to remember. The plus-size woman can look terrific in high-fashion looks providing the style lines and details are in proportion to her large body type and fit is impeccable. To help visualize the impact this customer can make in high-fashion styles, I have selected designs from leading designers and have interpreted them in the proportion of the plus-size body type.

47

Pierre Cardin, 1987

Valentino, 1987

The correct use of color can help the eye see not so much a large woman, but a well-dressed woman. These designs illustrate the use of harmonious and contrasting colors for the plus-size figure. Harmonious colors in prints (**1**) are best for the plus-size woman, because they do not call attention to themselves. Contrasting colors (**2** and **3**) break up horizontal lines and create vertical illusions.

1

2

3

4

5

6

A color theme evolves with styles made from the same fabric and color. It offers the plus-size woman a range of style choices for the most flattering results to suit her body type. These designs from Albert Nipon Dimensions illustrate how colors of the same intensity work together, how contrasting and harmonizing colors in a print convey one-color illusion.

50

Single-unit items should adhere to a color story and silhouette theme. Albert Nipon Dimensions favors red as the
fashion color and uses it in these examples in different
variations: in the same fabric with smooth vertical lines
(**7**), and in different fabrics and textures (**8**).

TWEED FANCY: PEACOCK CO; GARNET CO.

P#1923
PP#3923
PII#7923
PRICE:

MELTON: PEACOCK; GARNET;

P#1921
PP#7921
PII#7921
PRICE:

ART DECO PLAID: PEACOCK CO.

P#1966
PP#3966
PII#7966
PRICE:

TEXTURED FOULARD: GARNET/ NAVY CO.

P#1967
PP#3967
PII#7967
PRICE:

CREPE DE CHINE: WINTER WHITE; AQUAMARINE; GARNET

P#1960
PP#3960

P#1961
PP#3961

PII#7960
PRICE:

PII#7961
PRICE:

CDC W/LACE: WINTER WHITE ONLY

P#1962
PP#

P#1963
PP#3963

PII#7962
PRICE:

PII#7963
PRICE:

BRUSHSTROKE: PEACOCK CO.; GARNET CO.

P#1968
PP#3968
PII#7968
PRICE:

MEDALLION: NAVY CO.

P#1969
PP#3969
PII#7969
PRICE:

SKIN JACQUARD: WINTER WHITE; AQUAMARINE; GARNET

BRUSHSTROKE: PEACOCK CO.; GARNET CO.

MEDALLION: NAVY CO.

MIR PAISLEY: PEACOCK/GARNET/NAVY CO.

P#1930
PP#3930
PII#7930
PRICE:

CK GEOMETRIC: PEACOCK/GARNET/NAVY CO.

P#1931
PP#3931
PII#7931
PRICE:

FOULARD BORDER: PEACOCK CO.; GARNET CO.

Personal
Personal Petites
PERSONAL II

Separate Options

Brights

Fall I 1987

9

Leslie Fay Companies creates several color themes in fabrics to achieve one color dressing, color accent, color contrast and color harmony for the most flattering results. Group lines are planned around fabric and a color theme in a variety of styles becoming to each of the plus-size body types.

10

Vertical stripes in light neutral colors lengthen and thin
the figure, especially when contrasted with a dark skirt
(11).

11

A black and white bold print (**14**) with black contrasting velvet details at the shoulders and neckline gives the illusion of height and adds width to the shoulders. Color as an accent will attract the eye and when used near the face will divert attention from large hips (**12** and **13**), but *remember* use it sparingly.

12

13

14

15

16

Albert Nipon Dimensions combines a bold treatment of accent color across shoulders with a neutral background print to create an equalizing effect for the plus-size with a small bust and large hips (15). Both designs illustrate how the use of dark colors will absorb light and diminish size.

Arnold Scaasi, 1987

Giorgio Armani, 1987

Valentino, 1987

Yves Saint Laurent, 1987

Valentino, 1987

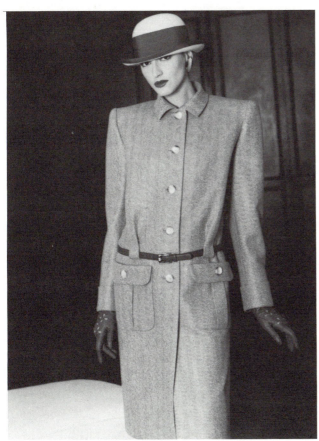

Yves Saint Laurent, 1987

Dior, 1987

Valentino, 1987

Dior, 1987

Ralph Lauren, 1987

Valentino, 1987

Dior, 1987

Giorgio Armani, 1987

James Galanos, 1987

Part Two

The successful interpretation of original designs into finished garments for all figure types is realized through the techniques of draping and/or flat pattern-making. Draping offers endless opportunities for expressing one's creativity. Draping is the molding of fabric to the rounded human figure represented by the dress form, using darts, tucks, seams and other style details. Draping requires the skillful use of your hands, palms and fingertips to gently smooth and manipulate fabric on grain in an upward, downward, inward and outward motion on the dress form.

Flat patternmaking is the drawing of a pattern on a flat surface to individual or standard measurements in a given size by applying the principles of drafting. *Sloper* is the popular term used for the basic bodice, skirt and sleeve patterns from which all designs are developed. Slopers are also called *master patterns, block patterns* or *foundation patterns*.

Pattern designs developed from flat patternmaking techniques will be cold, set and lifeless unless one has a knowledge of draping and has had experience in working with fabric on the dress form. Although flat pattern designs are accurate, they will not have the finer line placement gained through draping. Proportion of the garment as it relates to the human body and the effect of the fabric as it hangs on the human body are readily apparent when developing a pattern using draping methods. There is also an improvement of fit when flat pattern designs are made from a sloper and then draped on a dress form. The design quality of your designs will improve with a clear-cut understanding of draping. On the other hand, an understanding of flat patternmaking will assist you in accomplishing pattern designs with speed and accuracy. Combining both methods has the advantage of designing with greater creativity, freedom, efficiency and skill.

As with all methods, the fundamental principles must be learned before continuing. There are two basic considerations needed to drape effectively and efficiently: a knowledge of the anatomy of the human figure and the working properties of the fabric with which one works. The designer works with fabric or muslin to interpret an original idea. Fabric, which is two-dimensional, must be translated to a garment for

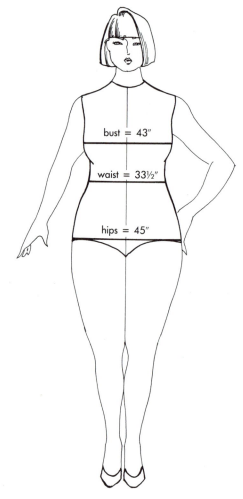

FIGURE 6-1

a human figure, which is three-dimensional. The fabric must take shape and form. It will be used to suggest and inspire occasions and silhouettes. Not all fabrics are appropriate for all occasions and silhouettes (fabric textures are discussed in detail on **page 29**).

The first principle to understand is the analysis of the human figure in relation to the needs for comfort, freedom and motion (**Figure 6-1**). This is necessary as draping is done on a dress form that duplicates the human figure but it cannot breathe, move, or bend arms and legs. The dress form represents the specification measurements of the manufacturer's sample size with ease added for chest, waist and hip expansion.

It is important to recognize the three divisional points of the human figure and dress form—*bust level, waist level,* and *hip level.* I often refer to them as the levels of control (**Figures 6-3, 6-4**). These levels of control will determine the silhouette, fit and ease of your design.

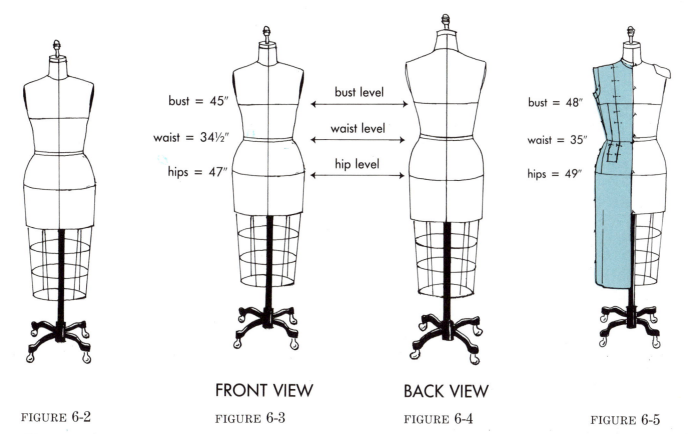

bust = 45"

waist = 34½"

hips = 47"

bust level

waist level

hip level

bust = 48"

waist = 35"

hips = 49"

FRONT VIEW

BACK VIEW

FIGURE 6-2   FIGURE 6-3   FIGURE 6-4   FIGURE 6-5

All the figures represent the same size. Note the difference in bust, waist and hip measurements. The dress form (Figure 6-3) measures 2 inches more around the bust, 1 inch more around the waist and 2 inches more around the hips than the human figure (Figure 6-1). The dress pattern (Figure 6-5) measures 3 inches more around the bust, ½ inch more around the waist and 2 inches more around the hips. The additional ease is necessary to have freedom in body movements.

The next important principle is an understanding of grain and the working properties of the fabric selected for your design.

At this point, I should explain the word *grain*. Grain, as it is defined in fashion, is the direction of the fibers that form the fabric. Woven fabric is composed of two sets of yarns (threads) that run at right angles to each other. The lengthwise yarn runs vertically to form the *lengthwise grain*. The *selvage* is the narrow, tightly woven lengthwise finished edge on each side of the fabric. Yarns that run horizontally from selvage to selvage form the *crosswise grain*. The fibers are strongest in the length direction and weakest in the crosswise direction. If one were to pull in a diagonal direction there is a certain amount of stretch. This diagonal stretch is referred to as the *bias grain*. A fabric is *on grain* when the lengthwise and crosswise threads run exactly at right angles to each other (**Figure 6-9**).

A finished garment made in fabric that is grain perfect keeps its shape, hangs and wears well, and fits perfectly. Thus, the first important step in draping patterns is to prepare the fabric to grain perfection. The fabric most often used in design rooms to drape patterns is called *muslin*. Muslin is a plain-weave fabric made from bleached or unbleached carded yarns in a variety of weights. The direction of the grain is easily visible and it can be marked with black and colored pencils. A pattern draped in muslin can be used repeatedly, and its relatively low cost makes it appropriate for experimenting and developing designs.

Procedure for Grain Perfect Muslin

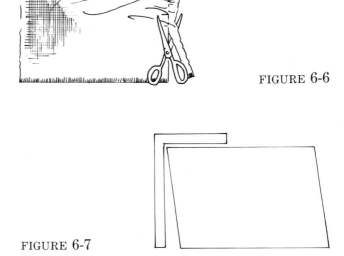

FIGURE 6-6

All fabrics are woven grain perfect with lengthwise and crosswise grains at right angles to each other. However, fabric may be temporarily pulled out of shape in the manufacturing process. To determine whether or not the fabric is grain perfect, it must be torn or cut on the crosswise grain from selvage to selvage on both ends. Thread perfect ends are essential for grain perfect fabric.

Figure 6-6

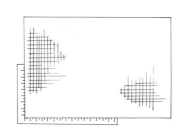

FIGURE 6-7

If muslin ends are not cut on grain, adjust by tearing or pulling one of the woven threads. Cut on the pulled thread line. As one develops expertise, muslin can be cut freehand on grain by visually following the weave of the crosswise thread. Fabric is thread perfect when a single thread runs across the cut or torn edge from selvage to selvage.

Figure 6-7

In this illustration grains are thread perfect on all four sides but are not on grain. Block muslin until lengthwise and crosswise grains are at *perfect* right angles to each other. Pull muslin in the direction shown in **Figure 6-8.**

FIGURE 6-8

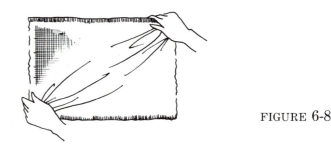

Figure 6-8 Blocking Muslin

Pull muslin ends diagonally in the direction needed until the lengthwise and crosswise grains are at right angles to each other.

FIGURE 6-9

Figure 6-9

Muslin is blocked, pressed and ready for draping.

FIGURE 6-10

Figure 6-10 Bias Grain

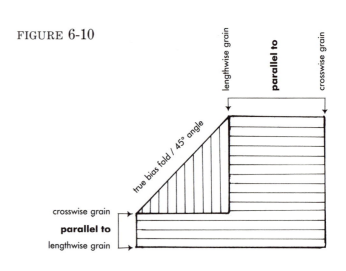

lengthwise grain

parallel to

crosswise grain

true bias fold / 45° angle

crosswise grain

parallel to

lengthwise grain

Relating Grain to the Levels of Control

When draping original designs, knowing the correct position of grain at the levels of control will result in the accurate and professional production of patterns. Each grain position will give a definite effect and fit.

Figure 6-11

Grain pinned straight across (parallel to the floor) at the bust level will result in fullness above and below the bust level.

Figure 6-12

Grain placed straight and smooth across the chest above the bust level will cause the grain to drop at the sides and all fullness will be below bust level.

Figure 6-13

Grain pinned smooth across the waistline will raise the grain upward at the sides of the bust level and all fullness will be above the bust level.

There are two standing orders or routine procedures for draping all patterns: only *one-half* of a pattern is draped using the *right side* of the dress form. Also draping patterns is divided into three procedures:

1. Preparing the fabric (muslin) before draping

2. Draping and marking the fabric (muslin) on the dress form

3. Trueing and pinning the draped pattern

When you've mastered the above principles, you'll avoid working by trial and error. A knowledge of *whys* can lead to a scientific approach to problem solving. The material covered in this unit, carefully applied, will result in the accurate and professional production of patterns for the plus-size figure.

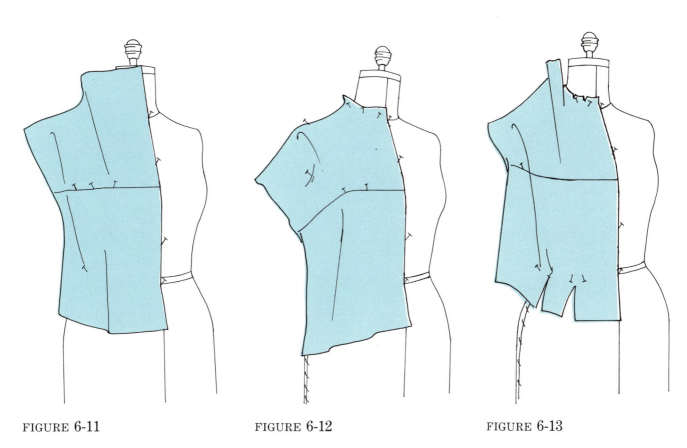

FIGURE 6-11   FIGURE 6-12   FIGURE 6-13

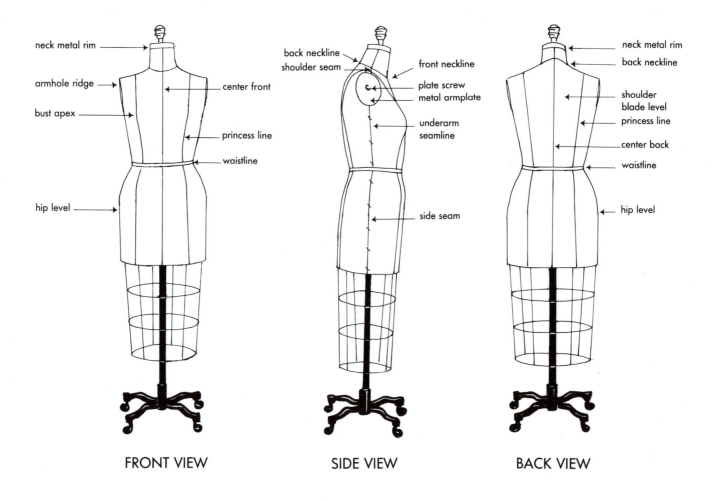

FRONT VIEW   SIDE VIEW   BACK VIEW

FIGURE 6-14   The dress form is a duplication of the human figure covered in a heavy linen-type fabric and set on a moveable height adjustable stand. It may be referred to as model or figure form. All seamlines are indicated on the dress form. Seamlines for center front, center back, neckline, shoulder, armhole, princess line and side seams are easily recognized.

Tools & Equipment

Tapemeasure

A narrow metal-tipped 60-inch woven or plastic tape, best for measuring the dress form or human figure.

Scissors

Two are needed. One good quality, at least 9 inches in length, for cutting fabric only and one for cutting paper since paper will dull scissors.

Pins

Size 17 steel satin straight pins, best for draping and fittings.

Pencils

Number 2 lead pencils to mark muslin, and red and blue pencils to make corrections.

Rulers

A clear plastic straight edge ruler 2″ × 18″ with squared lines at one-eighth intervals with ¼″, ½″ and 1″ measurements easily recognized.

L Square

A metal L-shaped ruler with one short side, 14 inches, and a longer side, 24 inches, used to check and establish grainlines at right angles.

French Curve

A clear plastic tool shaped into a curve at one end. Used to mark armholes and necklines.

Hip Curve

A metal 24-inch shallow curved ruler used to mark curved lines.

Style Tape

Narrow woven black tape to contrast with muslin, and used to establish style lines on muslin.

Tracing Wheel

A small hand tool with a serrated or pointed wheel at one end. Used to transfer markings from one side to another. The small serrated wheel is used on fabric.

Tracing Paper

Waxed carbon paper made for the garment industry. Red and blue are used to transfer pattern lines on muslin. White is used on fabrics.

An endless variety of designs can be developed from the basic bodice with shoulder and waistline darts sloper. The basic bodice is draped using the principles of the fundamental dart. Darts, whether they become tucks, pleats, shirring or folds, assist a two-dimensional fabric take form on a three-dimensional figure. Darts always radiate outward from the apex of the bust on the front, and from the shoulder and shoulder blades on the back.

Preparing Muslin for the Front Bodice

1. Estimate yardage (**Figure 7-1**).

    Lengthwise Grain Measure from the top neck rim of the dress form at center front to waistline plus 5 inches.

    Crosswise Grain Measure across bust level from underarm seam to center front plus 5 inches.

2. Cut muslin thread perfect on the lengthwise and crosswise grains the amount measured (see **Figures 6-6, 6-7, page 70**).

3. Block muslin until grain perfect and press (**Figures 6-8, 6-10, page 70**).

4. Identify grainlines.

    A. Fold length of muslin in half. This is the *bust level*. Identify crosswise grain across bust level in pencil. (**Figure 7-1**)

    B. Measure in 1 inch from the cut lengthwise edge and identify the center front lengthwise grain in pencil. (**Figure 7-1**)

    C. On the dress form, determine apex of the bust and place a pin. Measure distance from center front to apex and from apex to underarm seam.

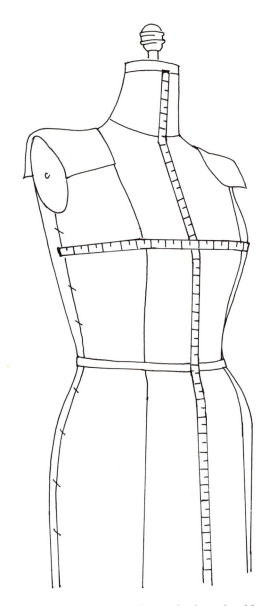

Plus-size proportions are enhanced when shoulder pads are used, therefore, drape all patterns with shoulder pads correctly positioned on the dress form.

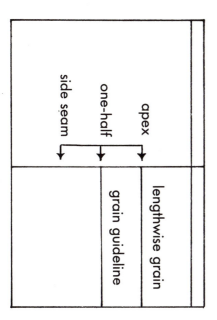

FIGURE 7-2

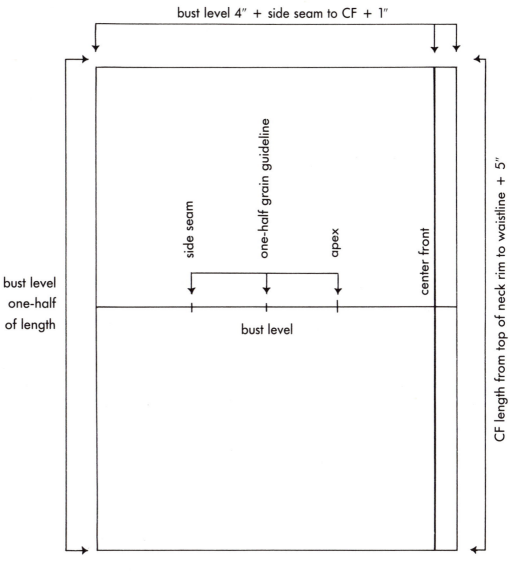

width measurement

bust level 4″ + side seam to CF + 1″

side seam

one-half grain guideline

apex

center front

bust level
one-half
of length

bust level

CF length from top of neck rim to waistline + 5″

FIGURE 7-1

D. On muslin identify the distance from center front to apex at the bust level crosswise grain with a pencil crossmark, divide in half the distance from apex to side seam plus ¼ inch ease and crossmark (**Figure 7-1**) (This crossmark will identify the placement for a grain guideline.)

E. Identify with pencil the lengthwise grain from the bust level to the bottom edge of muslin at apex and grain guideline crossmarks. (**Figure 7-2**)

Draping the Front Bodice

1. Fold under the 1-inch extension at center front, and crease lightly with fingers.

2. Place center front fold of muslin to center front of dress form at bust level with crosswise grain parallel to floor. Pin at apex, smooth muslin across chest and upward toward neckline; pin at center front neckline. Place a second pin at center front between bust level and neckline. (**Figure 7-3**)
   Note To secure muslin to dress form, sink point of pin through muslin into dress form diagonally with point of pin aimed inward toward muslin being draped.

3. Continue to pin center front muslin fold to dress form between bust level and waistline maintaining crosswise grains parallel to floor. (**Figure 7-3**)

4. Be sure muslin is smooth (there should be no appearance of diagonal pulls in the muslin above or below bust level). Muslin should not indent with center front of dress form at bust level. When the crosswise grain is straight, parallel to floor, there will be air space between the muslin and center front of dress form at bust level.

5. Drape muslin so that crosswise grain at bust level is straight across and the lengthwise

grains below bust level hang like a box at right angles to the crosswise grain. Pin on bust level between apex and underarm seam taking and pinning ease, ⅛ inch on double. Pin at underarm seam. (**Figures 7-3, 7-4**)

6. Smooth muslin at neckline, keeping grains at right angles to each other. Pin neckline midway between center front and shoulder. Slash diagonally, from top edge of muslin at center front to midway pin stopping ½ inch above neckline seam of dress form. (**Figure 7-3**)

7. Smooth muslin along shoulder; pin at princess seam of dress form. Pencil mark a vertical crossmark at pin (the princess seamline of shoulder). (**Figure 7-3**)

8. To determine depth of waistline dart, follow with point of pin penciled lengthwise guideline between apex and underarm seam gently straight down to waistline (bottom of tape) and pin. Slash up guideline from bottom edge of muslin to ½ inch of waistline seam. (**Figure 7-5**)

9. With back of hand gently smooth muslin at armplate and underarm seam down to waistline and pin. (**Figure 7-5**)
   Note There should be a pinch of ease (¹⁄₁₆ inch on double) between grain guideline and underarm seam at waistline when grain guideline is draped straight and underarm seam has been accurately pinned at waistline. (**Figure 7-5**)

10. Lightly crease muslin on apex grainline down to waistline. Excess muslin forms waistline dart. Pin dart at waistline vertically with the center of dart, the creased fold, extending outward. (**Figure 7-5**)

11. To drape shoulder dart crease, lightly crossmark at princess seam and direct fold toward apex. At armhole/shoulder intersection hold edge of muslin upward and smooth down over shoulder. Smooth excess muslin toward and under crease to form shoulder dart. Pin muslin to the dress form at arm-

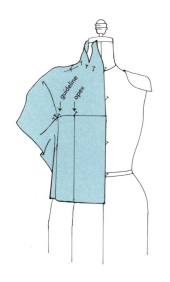

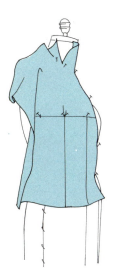

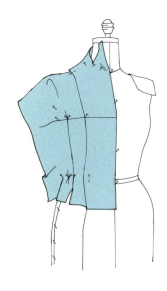

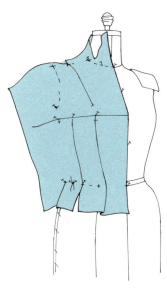

FIGURE 7-3　　　　　FIGURE 7-4　　　　　FIGURE 7-5　　　　　FIGURE 7-6

hole/shoulder intersection. Pin dart closed at shoulder with its under depth folded inward toward center front. (**Figure 7-5**)
Rule Place pins head to point at right angles to a fold. (**Figure 7-5**)

12. Pin vanishing point of shoulder and waistline darts.

13. **Marking the muslin.** The following must be marked accurately with a sharp pointed pencil before muslin is removed from the dress form in preparation for trueing.

   A. **Neckline** Crossmark (a horizontal dash ⅛-inch long) neckline at center front intersection and along neckline at inch intervals to shoulder. Crossmark at neckline and shoulder intersection. (**Figure 7-6**)
   Note Be sure crossmarks placed on muslin follow the direction of corresponding seams of dress form.

   B. **Shoulder** Crossmark across both sides of pinned dart. Place vertical marks on both

sides of pinned dart. Crossmark shoulder/armhole ridge intersections. (**Figure 7-6**)
Note The shoulder and armhole ridge is *not* the metal armplate of the dress form. The ridge is the edge of the dress form at shoulder and armhole to just above the level of the armplate screw.

   C. **Armhole** Mark armhole ridge from shoulder to just above the armplate screw level. Crossmark intersection of armplate and underarm seam and at short intervals mark armplate to screw level. (**Figure 7-6**)
   Note There will be approximately ⅛- to ¼-inch difference between ridge and armplate markings.

   D. **Waistline** Crossmark intersection of underarm seam at waistline (bottom of tape) and mark from underarm seam to waistline dart at short intervals. Crossmark waistline across both sides of dart and vertical crossmarks on either side. Crossmark vanishing points of shoulder and waistline darts. (**Figure 7-6**)

Trueing the Front Bodice

Even though patterns are carefully draped all lines that should be straight or curved must be trued using straight or curved rulers or any other necessary tool. Trueing is the process of connecting all points on a pattern and checking the accuracy of measurements made during draping or drafting the pattern such as dartlines, seamlines, crossmarks, shapes of seamlines.

1. Remove muslin from dress form removing all pins. Be sure you have not forgotten any essential marks. (**Figure 7-7**)

2. True waistline dart connecting vanishing point to either side of waistline dart, extending lines beyond waistine to end of muslin. (**Figure 7-8**)

3. True shoulder dart by connecting crossmark nearest neckline to apex at bust level. Connect shoulder crossmark nearest the armhole to vanishing point level on trued dartline. (**Figure 7-8**)

4. True underarm seam by connecting crossmarks at armplate and waistline with a straight line. To allow ease needed for a set-in sleeve the armhole is lowered and ease is added to the underarm seam. Lower armhole 1½ inches from armplate, crossmark at underarm seam. At lowered armhole square a line out ½ inch from the underarm seam and connect to waistline and underarm seam intersection crossmark with straight line. (**Figure 7-8**)

5. To true armhole, position french curve so that the deepest curve touches the lower 1½-inch level of the lowered armhole, and the outside edge aligns with shoulder and armhole intersection crossmark and armhole ridge marks or falls between the marks at the plate screw level. (**Figure 7-8**)

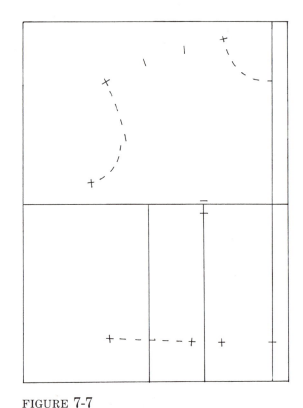

FIGURE 7-7

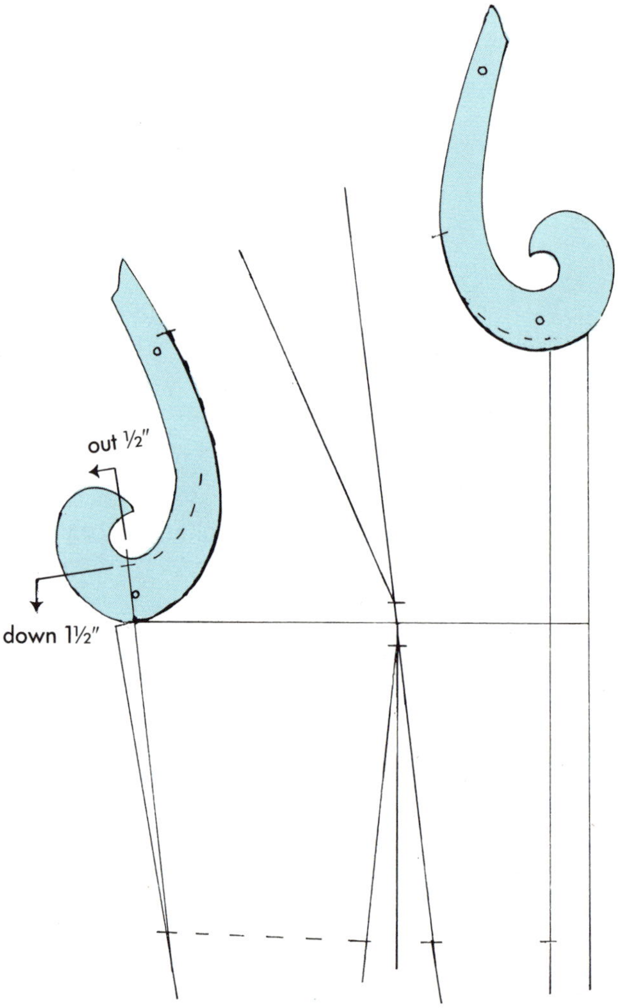

out ½"

down 1½"

FIGURE 7-8

6. To true neckline, follow crosswise grain at right angles to center front at neckline ¼ to ½ inch (this is to avoid a pointed shape (∧), to the neckline seam at center front). Position french curve edge to blend neckline marks so that it touches the crossmark at neck and shoulder intersection. True curved neckline. (**Figure 7-8**)

7. To true shoulder seam crease the dartline nearest the center front and bring this line to meet the dartline nearest the armhole, pin dart closed beginning at vanishing point to shoulder seam intersection. (**Figure 7-10**) **Note** All pins should be inserted at the folded seam edge through all three layers of muslin and at right angles to the seamline. Pin pick-up should be not more than ⅛ inch. With dart pinned closed true shoulder seam, using straight ruler connect crossmarks at neckline and armhole ridge in straight line. (**Figure 7-9**)

8. Add ½ inch seam allowance at neckline, 1 inch at shoulder and the ease extended underarm seamline. Cut excess muslin. Cut armhole roughly leaving 2 inches at underarm seam to 1½ inch at plate screw level and shoulder seam. (**Figure 7-10**))

9. To pin waistline dart closed, crease dartline lightly nearest center front and bring the creased line to meet dartline nearest underarm seam. Pin dart closed beginning at vanishing point and ending at waistline crossmark (follow directions for pinning in **Step 7 Note**). (**Figure 7-10**)

10. Return front bodice to dress form being careful that all marks are accurately pinned to dress form. At shoulder seam sink pins completely into dress form so that seam allowance is held flat and molded to dress form. Repeat for underarm seam.

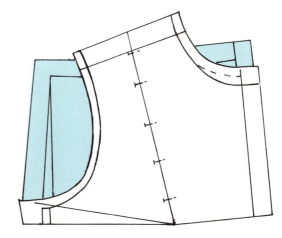

FIGURE 7-9

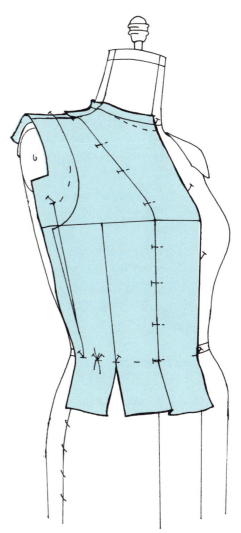

FIGURE 7-10

79

Preparing Muslin for the Back Bodice

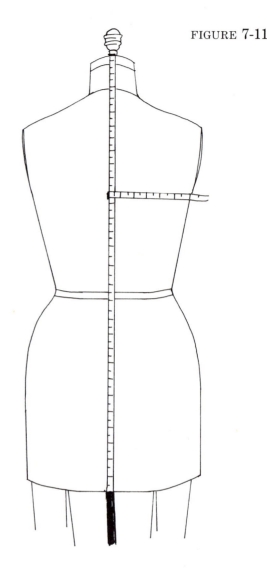

FIGURE 7-11

1. Estimate yardage (**Figure 7-11**).

   Lengthwise Grain Measure from the top neck rim of the dress form at center back to waistline plus 5 inches.

   Crosswise Grain Measure across bust level from underarm seam to center back plus 5 inches.

2. Cut muslin thread perfect on the lengthwise and crosswise grains the amount measured (see **Figures 6-6, 6-7, page 70**).

3. Block muslin until grain perfect and press (**Figures 6-8, 6-9, page 70**).

4. Identify grainlines. (**Figure 7-12**)

   A. Measure in 1 inch from the cut lengthwise edge and identify the center back lengthwise grain in pencil (**Figure 7-12**).

   B. Fold under the 1 inch extension at center back and crease lightly with fingers.

   C. Place center back fold of muslin to center back of dress form, with top edge at neck rim, pin center back at neckline down to waistline. Crossmark center back at neckline and waistline.

   Remove muslin from dress form.

   D. Fold muslin at center back in half from neckline to waistline crossmarks. Bring neckline crossmark at center back to halfway fold and crossmark. This is the shoulder blade level (the top one-quarter center back length from neckline to waistline). Identify with pencil the crosswise grain across the muslin at the shoulder blade level. (**Figure 7-13**)

   E. On the dress form, measure distance across shoulder blade level from center back to armplate.

   F. On muslin, identify the distance from center back to armplate plus ¼ inch ease and crossmark. (**Figure 7-14**)

   H. At shoulder blade level measure in from armplate crossmark (toward center back) 1¼ inches, crossmark to identify the placement of a grain guidance. (**Figure 7-13**).

   I. Identify with pencil the lengthwise grain from shoulder blade level, at grain guideline crossmark to bottom edge of muslin. (**Figure 7-13**)

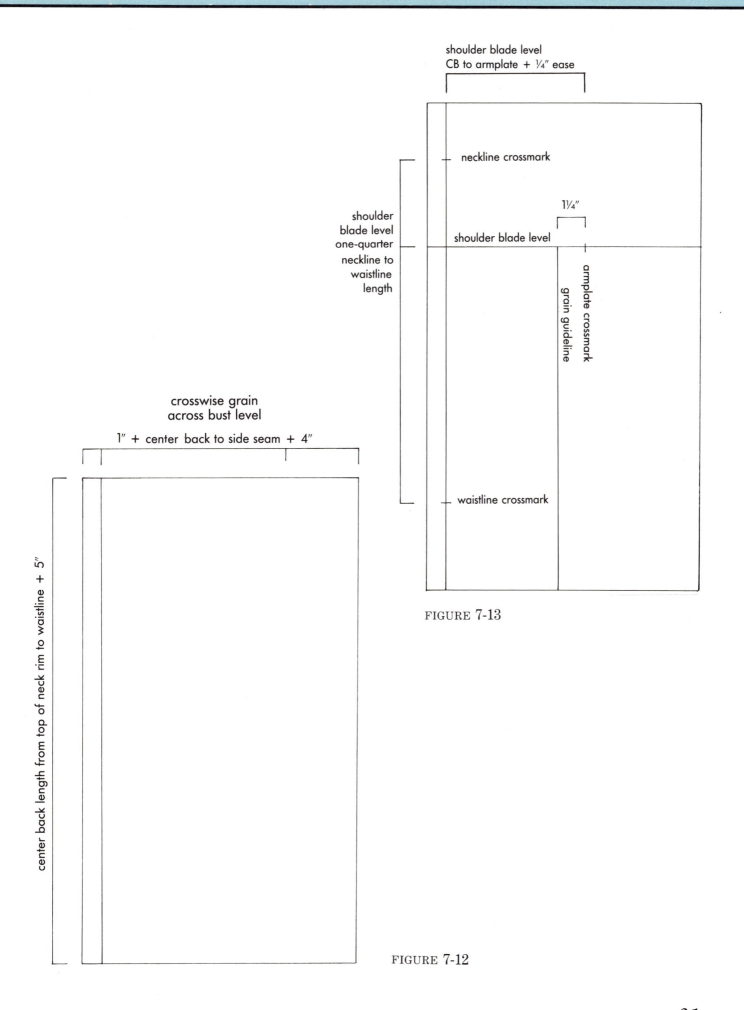

shoulder blade level
CB to armplate + ¼" ease

neckline crossmark

1¼"

shoulder blade level

shoulder
blade level
one-quarter
neckline to
waistline
length

armplate crossmark

grain guideline

waistline crossmark

FIGURE 7-13

crosswise grain
across bust level

1" + center back to side seam + 4"

center back length from top of neck rim to waistline + 5"

FIGURE 7-12

Draping the Back Bodice

1. Pin center back fold of muslin to center back of dress form at neckline, shoulder blade level and waistline. Be sure to secure pins (see Draping Front Bodice, **Step 2 Note**).

2. Smooth crosswise grain across shoulder blade level. Pin crosswise grain across shoulder blade level to armplate parallel to floor, taking and pinning ⅛ inch ease on double, before grain guideline. Pin at armplate and underarm seam. (**Figure 7-15**)

3. To establish the depth of waistline dart, smooth grain guideline at shoulder blade level with point of pin down straight to waistline and pin. Slash guideline from bottom edge of muslin to ½ inch of waistline seam. (**Figure 7-15**)
   Note It is important that the dart depth vanish below the bust level. When dart vanishes above bust level, it is too deep. Check and adjust grain guideline to be sure it is falling straight at right angles to shoulder blade level (move toward underarm seam to correct).

4. With back of hand, gently smooth muslin at armplate and underarm seam down to waistline and pin. (**Figure 7-15**)
   Note There should be a pinch of ease (¹⁄₁₆ inch on double) between grain guideline and underarm seam at waistline when grain guideline is draped straight and underarm seam has been pinned accurately at waistline.

5. From center back waistline mark the same distance of front waistline dart to center front with a vertical crossmark that intersects waistline. (**Figure 7-15**)

6. Crease dart crossmark, smooth excess muslin under crease to form waistline dart. Pin dart at waistline pinning through three layers of muslin and at right angles to waistline.

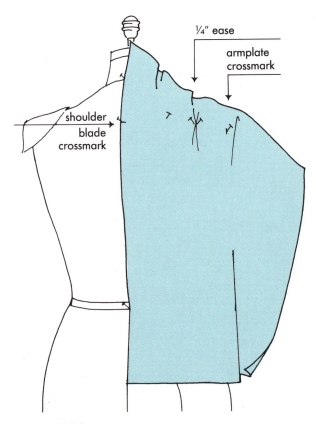

FIGURE 7-14

Pin pick-up should be no more than ⅛ inch. (**Figure 7-20**)

7. Crossmark vanishing point of waistline dart. For correct fit it is essential that dart vanishes below bust level. (**Figure 7-16**)

8. Smooth muslin at neckline, keeping grains at right angles to each other. Pin neckline midpoint from center back to shoulder seam. Slash from top edge of muslin toward neckline midpoint pin, stopping ½ inch above neckline seam. Smooth muslin across neckline and up to shoulder intersection, slash and pin as necessary. (**Figure 7-16**)

9. To determine ease and depth of shoulder dart, drape muslin at shoulder blade level and armplate, up toward front shoulder and pin. (**Figure 7-16**)

10. Smooth muslin across shoulder taking a pinch of ease midway between neckline and front shoulder dart and midway between armhole and front shoulder dart. (**Figure 7-17**)

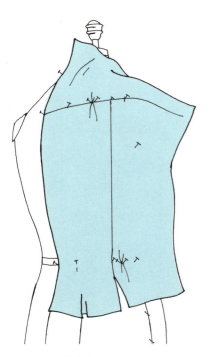

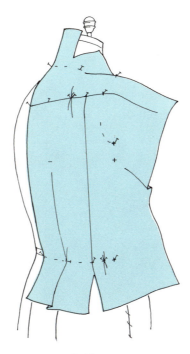

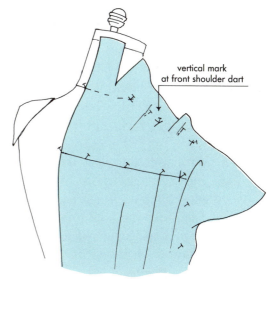

FIGURE 7-15   FIGURE 7-16   FIGURE 7-17

11. To form back shoulder dart fold on vertical crossmark and smooth excess fullness underneath. Pin dart at shoulder seam with dart depth folded inward toward center back. (**Figures 7-17, 7-18**)

12. **Marking the muslin. (Figures 7-16, 7-17, 7-18)**

   A. **Neckline** Crossmark at center back along neckline seam to shoulder and at shoulder neckline seam intersection.

   B. **Shoulder** Mark back shoulder seam directly over front shoulder seam at 1-inch intervals and across shoulder dart. Identify both sides of pinned shoulder dart with vertical crossmarks. Crossmark intersection at shoulder and armhole.

   C. **Armhole** Identify back muslin, armplate and underarm seam intersection and lowered armhole crossmarks directly from front bodice. Mark armplate at short intervals to plate screw level.

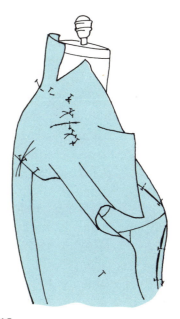

FIGURE 7-18

   D. **Waistline** Crossmark back underarm and waistline seam intersection directly from front muslin. Mark waistline (bottom of tape) from underarm seam to back waistline dart. Place vertical crossmarks at both sides of waistline dart. Be sure that vanishing point of back waistline dart has been marked.

83

Trueing the Back Bodice

1. Remove muslin from dress form. Be sure you have identified all necessary marks on muslin. (**Figure 7-19**) *Do not* remove pin at waistline dart intersection.

2. With waistline dart pinned closed at waistline seam, crease underneath fold with fingers (underneath crease is center of back waistline dart). Remove pin and identify with pencil lengthwise grain at crease from below waistline seam to vanishing point of dart. (**Figure 7-20**)

3. Using straight ruler connect crossmarks on both sides of waistline dart in a straight line to vanishing point at center grainline. (**Figure 7-20**)

4. Using straight ruler connect crossmark of shoulder dart nearest neckline and center back in a straight line to vanishing point of back waistline dart. Measure down from shoulder on this line 3 inches and crossmark, this becomes the vanishing point of shoulder dart. Connect the shoulder crossmark nearest the armhole to the vanishing point with a straight line. (**Figure 7-20**)

5. True neckline. (**Figure 7-20**)

   A. At center back pencil crosswise grain ½ inch toward shoulder.

   B. Position french curve to touch and blend marks to shoulder seam. True neckline to and beyond shoulder intersection.

6. True underarm seam. (**Figure 7-21**) Connect crossmarks at armplate and waistline intersection with straight line. To allow ease needed for a set in sleeve, at lowered armhole crossmark square a line out ½ inch from trued underarm seam and with straight ruler connect a line to waistline and underarm seam intersection.

7. True armhole. (**Figure 7-21**)

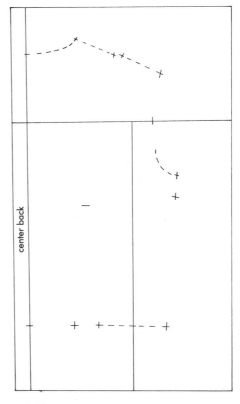

FIGURE 7-19

A. With straight ruler connect an armhole guideline from armplate crossmark at shoulder blade level to waistline and underarm seam intersection with a broken line in pencil.

B. Position french curve against guideline for approximately 2 inches from armplate crossmark at shoulder blade level, with deepest outside curve touching the lowered armhole crossmark, the outside edge aligns with shoulder and armhole intersection crossmark. True armhole line with french curve held steady in this position.
   Note It may not always be possible to true the complete armhole seam in one procedure. It may be necessary to blend armhole above shoulder blade level separately when french curve does not align with top armhole/shoulder intersection crossmark.

8. True shoulder. (**Figure 7-21**)

   A. Pin shoulder dart closed beginning at

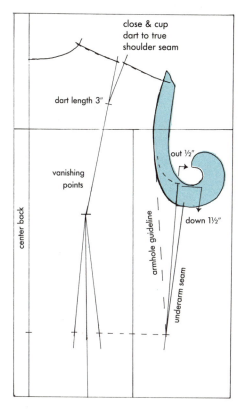

FIGURE 7-20

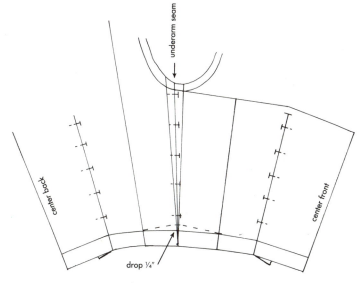

FIGURE 7-21

vanishing point bringing the side nearest neckline over to the side nearest armhole.

B. Using hip curve position to blend a shallow curve from shoulder and neckline intersection to shoulder dart and continue a nearly straight line from shoulder dart to armhole intersection. True shoulder seamline.

9. Add ½ inch seam allowance to neckline seam and 1 inch to shoulder and the ease extended underarm seamline. Cut excess.

10. True waistline. Before waistline seam can be trued, all darts and seams that intersect waistline of bodice must be pinned closed. (**Figure 7-21**)

A. To pin back waistline dart, crease lightly dartline nearest center back and bring the creased line to meet dartline nearest underarm seam. Pin dart closed beginning at vanishing points and stopping at waistline crossmark (see **Step 7, Note**).

B. Remove pinned front bodice from dress form.

C. Fold lightly the ease-extended line of underarm seam and bring fold to meet the ease-extended underarm seam of the front bodice. Match crossmarks of lowered armhole and waistline intersections. Pin underarm seams together.

D. At front waistline dart intersection follow crosswise grain with pencil to center front and from back waistline dart intersection to center back.

E. At underarm and waistline seam intersection ease is needed for arm motion. Measure down approximately ¼ inch at pinned underarm seam and blend with curve ruler to front and back waistline darts.

F. Blend dart intersections with gentle curve if needed. Add 1 inch seam allowance to waistline seam and cut excess muslin.

11. If needed blend armhole curve at underarm seam with the deep outside curve of french curve with a continuous well-shaped armhole line. Add ½ inch seam allowance to front and back armhole seam. Cut excess muslin.

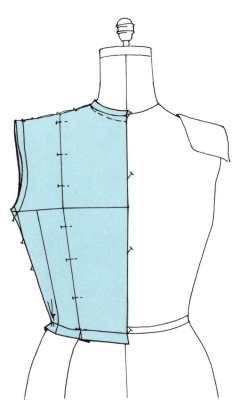

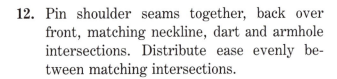

FIGURE 7-22

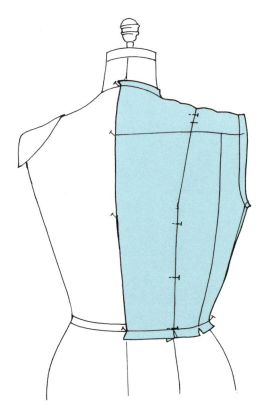

FIGURE 7-23

12. Pin shoulder seams together, back over front, matching neckline, dart and armhole intersections. Distribute ease evenly between matching intersections.

13. Return bodice to dress form for final checking. Pin front neckline and waistline at center front. Pin back neckline and waistline at center back. Check the general effect and appearance of the entire bodice from all angles. (**Figures 7-22, 7-23**)

　　A. There should not be any diagonal pulls in appearance.

B. The direction of all the darts should slant in toward the center from the shoulder to waistline.

C. Shoulder and underarm seams should appear straight.

D. There should be a minimum 1½ inch ease at bust level from center front to center back.

E. The shape of the armhole oval from the side view should be pleasing.

The draped basic skirt sloper serves as a foundation from which to design other skirts through the flat patternmaking method, and together with the draped basic bodice makes a master pattern from which to design the complete body of any desired garment.

In all straight skirts the side seams, hip level and hem run parallel to the grain and are either gathered, pleated, or darted to fit the waistline. The grain at hip level is always parallel to the floor. On the large-size figure the back waistline is best gathered or partially gathered using elastic for comfort and ease in movement.

Although the body shape differs from front to back, the method and principles of draping skirts for either is essentially the same.

Preparing Muslin for the Front Skirt

1. Estimate yardage (**Figure 8-1**).

   Lengthwise Grain Measure the desired length of skirt plus 4 inches.

   Crosswise Grain Measure across hip level from center front to side seam plus 5 inches.

2. Cut muslin thread perfect on the lengthwise and crosswise grains the amount measured.

3. Block muslin until grain perfect.

4. Identify grainlines on muslin (**Figure 8-1**).

   A. Measure in 1 inch from the cut lengthwise edge and identify the center front lengthwise grain in pencil.

   B. At the center front, measure down from the top edge and place crossmarks 2 inches and 9 inches below the top edge. The 2-inch crossmark establishes the waistline and the 9-inch crossmark represents the hip level which is 7 inches below waistline.

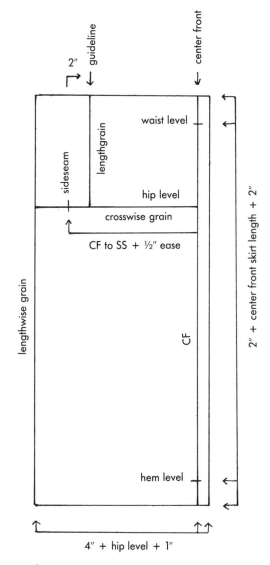

FIGURE 8-1

Note The hip level may be established anywhere from 7 to 9 inches below waistline depending on body type.

C. Identify crosswise grain across hip level in pencil.

D. On the dress form, measure at hip level the distance from center front to side seam plus ½ inch ease. On muslin place a crossmark to identify the side seam at hip level.

E. Measure in 2 inches from side seam crossmark (toward center front) and identify the lengthwise grain from hip level to top edge of muslin.

Draping the Front Skirt

1. Fold under the 1 inch extension at center front and crease lightly with fingers.

2. Place waistline crossmark at center front fold of muslin to the dress form at bottom of tape. Pin muslin at waistline, hip level and bottom of dress form. (**Figure 8-2**)

3. Smooth crosswise grain straight across hip level. Pin hip level to dress form at princess line, guideline, and side seam, taking ¼-inch ease on double between guideline and side seam. Be sure as you pin at side seam, the hip level is parallel to the floor and ease fold is directed diagonally toward the center front at bottom edge of muslin. Directing the ease as a fold diagonally toward center front will give a slenderizing effect to the basic skirt. (**Figure 8-2**)

4. To establish the depth of waistine darts, smooth guideline at hip level gently with point of pin straight up over hip bone to waistline and pin.

5. From center front waistline mark muslin at the princess line of the dress form with a vertical *crossmark* that *intersects* waistline. When draping the skirt with a bodice, position skirt dart nearest center front the same distance established between center front and waist dart on the basic front bodice. (**Figure 8-2**)

6. With back of hand, smooth muslin up at hip level from side seam to waistline and pin. (**Figure 8-3**)
   Note There should be a pinch of ease (1⁄16 inch on double) between grain guideline and side seam when grain guideline is draped straight and side seam has been accurately pinned at waistline.

7. Smooth crosswise grain across waistline from center front to crossmark and pin. Be sure muslin is smooth (there should be no appearance of diagonal pulls above or below hip level).

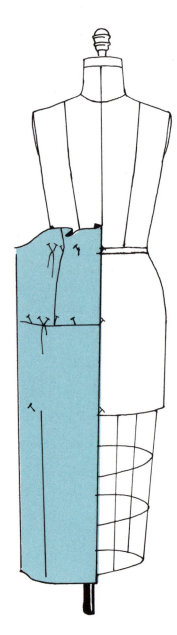

FIGURE 8-2

8. Divide excess fullness at waistline in half; pin and distribute fullness evenly to form two darts.

9. Pin dart nearest center front vertically at crossmark with center of dart extending outward.

10. With depth of second dart flat toward center front, measure and crossmark the midway point of waistline between the side seam and pinned dart nearest center front. (**Figure 8-4a**)

FIGURE 8-3

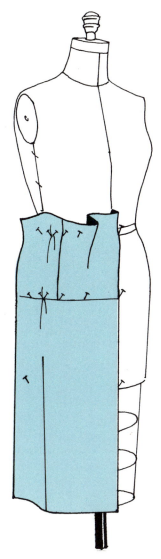

FIGURE 8-4

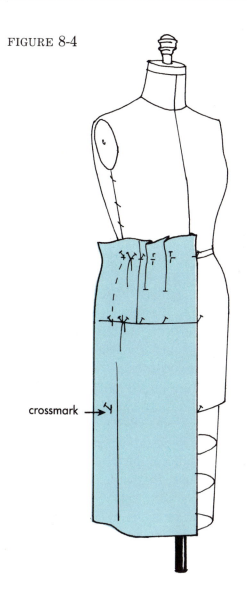

crossmark →

11. With midway crossmark as center, pin second dart at waistline. (**Figure 8-4a**)

12. Pin vanishing point of darts. Both darts vanish at the same level.

13. **Mark** accurately the following. (**Figure 8-4**)

   A. **Waistline** (bottom of tape) from side seam to center front. Be sure to mark across both sides of dart pins and intersect both sides of pin with vertical marks.

   B. **Side Seam** from hip level to waistline. Be sure to crossmark waistline and side seam intersection.

   C. **Crossmark** side seam at bottom of dress form torso.

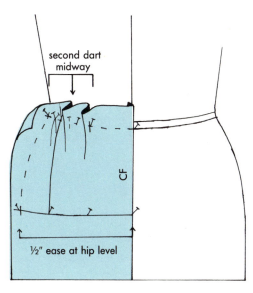

second dart
midway

CF

½" ease at hip level

FIGURE 8-4A

89

Trueing the Front Skirt

1. Remove muslin from dress form.

2. True lengthwise grain at center of each dart from waistline to vanishing point level, extending grainline to top edge of muslin. (**Figure 8-5**)

3. Place french curve with straighter outside curve touching crossmarks at waistline and vanishing point. True waistline darts extending line above waistline. (**Figure 8-6**)

4. Place hip curve with the deepest outside curve at the top, blend marks at side seam from hip level to waistline. True side seam from hip level to top edge of muslin. Follow lengthwise grain from hip level to bottom edge of muslin. (**Figure 8-6**)
   Note When mark indicating bottom of dress form torso is outside the trued lengthwise grainline (because thighs are wider than hips—pear-shape body type), connect and true a second straight line from hip level to bottom torso mark extending to bottom edge of muslin.

5. Add 1 inch seam allowance at side seam, cut excess.

6. Pin darts closed beginning at vanishing point and ending at waistline with dart depth folded inward to center front.

7. Return skirt front to dress form. Be sure all marks are accurately pinned to dress form. At side seam, sink pins completely into dress form to hold seam allowance flat.

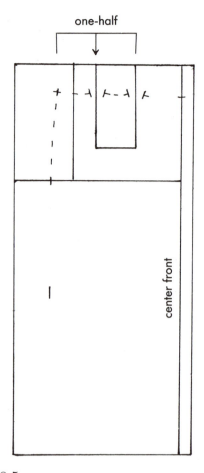

FIGURE 8-5

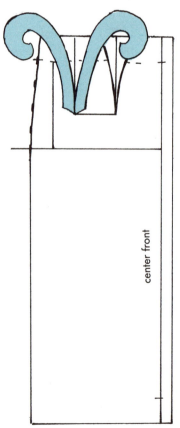

FIGURE 8-6

Preparing Muslin for the Back Skirt

1. Estimate yardage (**Figure** 8-7).

   Lengthwise Grain Same length as front skirt.

   Crosswise Grain Measure across hip level from center back to side seam plus 5 inches.

2. Cut muslin thread perfect on the lengthwise and crosswise grains the amount measured.

3. Block muslin until grain perfect.

4. Identify grainlines on muslin (**Figure** 8-7). See **Preparing Muslin for the Front Skirt, #4 A–E, page 87.**

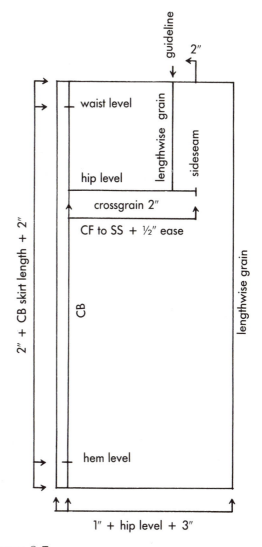

FIGURE 8-7

Draping the Back Skirt

1. Fold under the 1-inch extension at center back and crease lightly with fingers.

2. Place center back fold of muslin to back of dress form aligning hip level crosswise grain with hip level of front skirt at side seam. Pin hip level to dress form at center back, princess line, guideline and side seam taking ¼ inch ease on double between guideline and side seam. Be sure as you pin, the hip level is parallel to the floor and ease fold is directed diagonally to bottom edge of muslin inward toward center back. (**Figure 8-8**)

3. To establish depth of waistline dart or gathers, smooth guideline at hip level gently with point of pin straight up back to waistline and pin. (**Figure 8-9**)

4. With back of hand, smooth muslin up at hip level from side seam to waistline and pin taking a pinch of ease (¹⁄₁₆ inch on double between grain guideline and side seam). (**Figure 8-9**)

5. Distribute and pin excess fullness across waistline. (**Figure 8-9**)

6. **Mark** accurately the following. (**Figure 8-9**)

   A. Waistline/side seam intersection directly from front muslin and continue to mark bottom of tape to princess line of dress form.

   B. Mark directly from front muslin side seam from hip level to waistline; mark side seam at the bottom of dress form torso and crossmark bottom edge of front muslin.

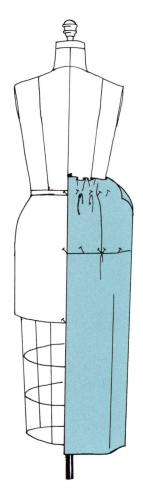

FIGURE 8-8

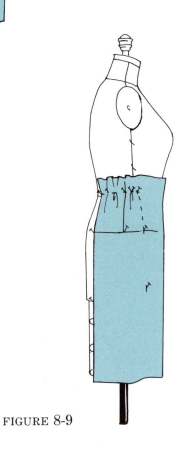

FIGURE 8-9

Trueing the Back Skirt

1. Remove back muslin from dress form. (**Figure 8-10**)

2. To true the side seam, position hip curve with the deeper outside curve at top, blend marks at side seam from hip level extending line to top edge of muslin and follow lengthwise grain from hip level to bottom edge of muslin. **Note** Grains at side seam of back skirt must balance with side seam of front skirt. When the side seam is not on straight grain, be sure the back seam is the same distance from the straight grain as the front side seam. (**Figure 8-11,** broken line)

3. Add 1 inch seam allowance and cut excess muslin.

4. Remove front skirt muslin from dress form.

5. Pin skirt muslins together at side seam, back over front, matching waistline and hip level crossmarks.

6. True waistline.

   A. With outside edge of hip curve touching waistline marks true a blended line from side seam to and across pinned darts of front skirt. At dart intersection nearest center front, follow crosswise grain across to center front. (**Figure 8-12**)

   B. With hip curve blend back waistline marks from side seam to princess seam area; follow crosswise grain across the center back. (**Figure 8-12**)

7. True hemline 2 inches above bottom edge of skirt and parallel to hip level. (**Figure 8-12**)

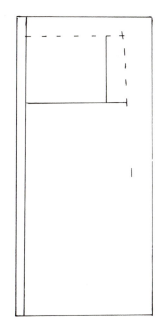
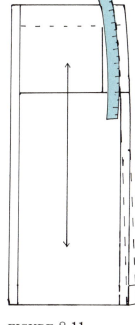

FIGURE 8-10   FIGURE 8-11

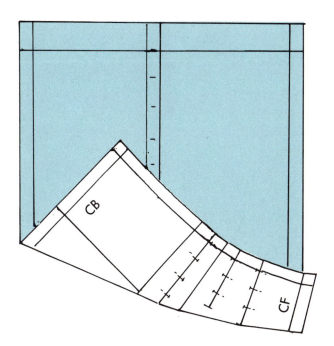

FIGURE 8-12

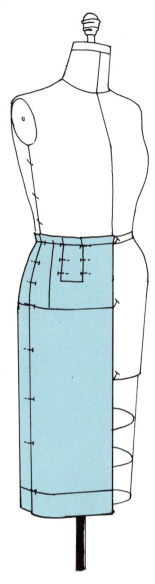

FIGURE 8-13

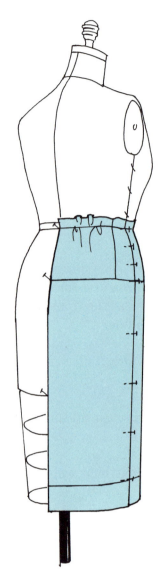

FIGURE 8-14

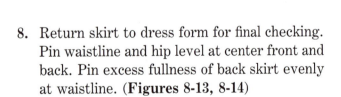

8. Return skirt to dress form for final checking. Pin waistline and hip level at center front and back. Pin excess fullness of back skirt evenly at waistline. (**Figures 8-13, 8-14**)

    A. The center front and center back lines should hang perpendicular to the floor.

    B. The side seam should fall perpendicular to the floor from hip level to lower edge.

    C. Crossmarks should match exactly.

    D. The hip level should be parallel to floor at all angles.

The shift is a one-piece dress without a waistline seam hanging straight from the shoulders. It is the best fitting foundation pattern for developing an endless variety of silhouettes and designs to enhance the plus-size figure. It is appropriate for the large-side body types as it allows for freedom of movement and conceals figure problems.

Preparing Muslin for the Front Shift

1. Estimate yardage. (**Figure 9-1**)

   Lengthwise Grain Measure from the top neck rim of the dress form at center front to waistline plus desired skirt length plus 2 inches.

   Crosswise Grain Measure across bust level (hip level if wider) from underarm seam to center front plus 5 inches.

2. Cut muslin thread perfect on the lengthwise and crosswise grains the amount measured.

3. Block muslin until grain perfect and press.

4. Identify grainlines.

   A. Measure in 1 inch from the cut lengthwise edge and identify the center front lengthwise grain in pencil.

   B. Fold under 1-inch extension at center front and crease lightly with fingers.

   C. Place center front fold of muslin to center front of dress form with crosswise grains parallel to floor; pin at neck, bust and hip level 7 inches below bottom of waistline tape. (**Figure 9-1**)

   D. Drape muslin crosswise grain straight across bust level from center front, pin at apex and underarm seam taking and pinning ease ⅛ inch on double between apex and underarm seam. (**Figure 9-1**)

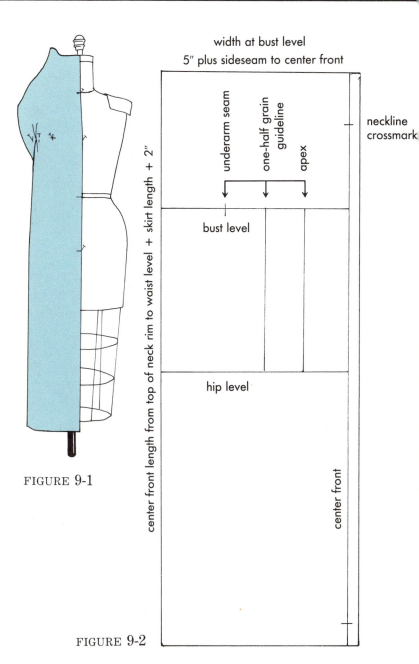

FIGURE 9-1

FIGURE 9-2

   E. Crossmark apex and bust level intersection and mark underarm. (**Figure 9-1**)

   F. Remove muslin from dress form.

   G. Identify bust level crosswise grain in pencil from apex to center front and across full width of muslin. (**Figure 9-2**)

   H. Identify crosswise grain across muslin from hip level crossmark at center front. (**Figure 9-2**)

   I. Identify lengthwise grain in pencil from bust level to hip level at apex and halfway from apex to underarm seam. (**Figure 9-2**)

95

Draping the Front Shift

1. Place center front fold of muslin to center front of dress form with crosswise grain parallel to floor at bust and hip level. Pin at apex, smooth muslin across chest and upward toward neckline, pin center front at neckline, midway between neckline and bust level, hip level and bottom of dress form torso. (**Figure 9-3**)

2. Be sure muslin is smooth (there should be no appearance of diagonal pulls in the muslin above or below bust level). Muslin should not indent with center front of dress form at bust level. When the crosswise grain is parallel to floor there will be air space between muslin and center front of dress form at bust level.

3. Smooth crosswise grain straight across bust level, pin grain guideline to dress form taking and pinning ease (⅛ inch on double), pin bust level at under seam. (**Figures 9-3, 9-4**)

4. Smooth crosswise grain straight across hip level parallel to floor. Pin hip level to dress form at apex guideline and side seam taking ¼ inch ease on double between grain guideline and side seam. Be sure as you pin at side seam, the ease fold at the bust level is directed diagonally toward the center front at bottom edge of muslin. Directing the ease from bust level and hip level as a fold diagonally toward center front, will have a slenderizing effect. (**Figures 9-3, 9-4**)

5. Smooth muslin at neckline, keeping grains at right angles to each other. Pin neckline midway between center front and shoulder. Slash diagonally from top edge of muslin at center front to midway pin stopping ½ inch above neckline seam of dress form. (**Figure 9-4**)

6. Smooth muslin along shoulder, pin and cross-mark princess seam of dress form. (**Figure 9-4**)

7. To drape shoulder dart crease lightly cross-

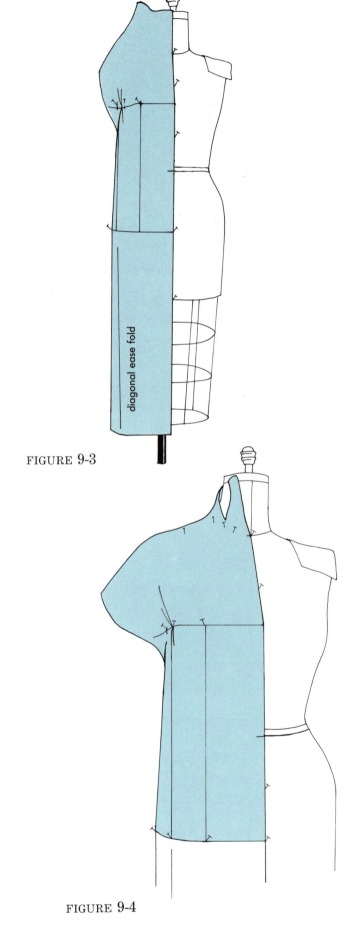

FIGURE 9-3

FIGURE 9-4

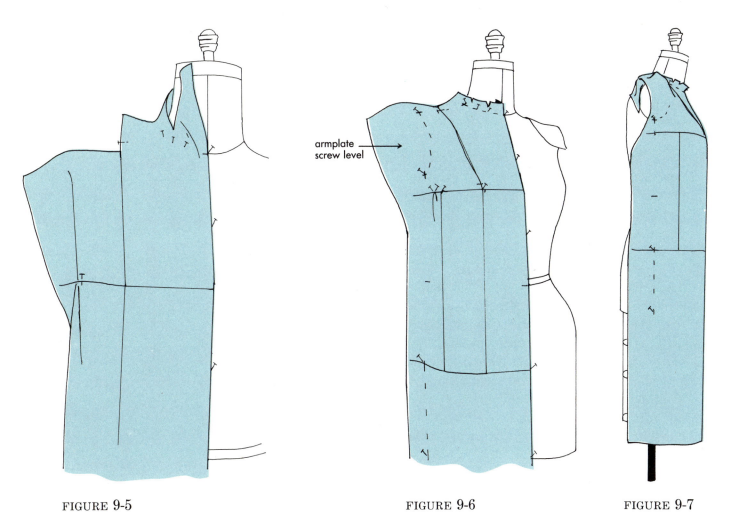

FIGURE 9-5   FIGURE 9-6   FIGURE 9-7

mark at princess seam and direct fold toward apex. (**Figure 9-5**) At armhole and shoulder intersection hold edge of muslin upward and smooth down over shoulder. Smooth excess muslin toward and under crease to form shoulder dart. Pin muslin to the dress form at armhole and shoulder intersection. Pin dart closed at shoulder with its under depth folded inward toward center front. Crossmark vanishing point of dart. (**Figure 9-6**)

8. **Mark: (Figures 9-6, 9-7)**

   A. **Neckline** Crossmark neckline at center front intersection and along neckline at inch intervals to shoulder. Crossmark neckline and shoulder intersection.

   B. **Shoulder** Crossmark across both sides of pinned dart. Place vertical marks on both sides of pinned dart. Crossmark shoulder and armhole ridge intersection.

   C. **Armhole** Mark the armhole ridge from shoulder to just above the armplate screw level. Crossmark intersection of armplate and underarm seam and at short intervals mark armplate to screw level.

   D. **Underarm Seam** Crossmark waistline. Mark underarm seam at short intervals from hip level to bottom edge of dress form torso.

97

Trueing the Front Shift

1. Remove muslin from dress form. Be sure all essential marks are identified on muslin.

2. True shoulder dart by connecting crossmark nearest neckline to apex at bust level. Connect shoulder crossmark nearest the armhole to vanishing point level on trued dartline. (**Figure 9-8**)

3. True underarm seam by connecting crossmarks from armplate to hip level with a straight line. To allow ease needed for a set in sleeve, lower armhole 1½ inches from armplate, crossmark at underarm seam. At lowered armhole crossmark square a line out ½ inch from underarm seam and connect to underarm seam at hip level with a straight line. From hip level to bottom edge of muslin, blend marks at side seam with a straight line. (**Figure 9-8**)

4. True neckline shoulder and armhole. Refer to **Trueing the Front Bodice, Steps 5 to 8.** (**Figure 9-8**)

5. Add seam allowances and cut excess muslin.

6. Return muslin to dress form and sink pins to hold seam allowances flat against dress form in preparation for draping the back shift. (**Figure 9-9**)

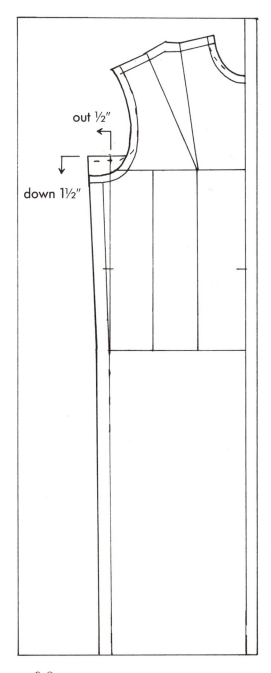

FIGURE 9-8

Preparing Muslin for the Back Shift

1. Estimate yardage.

   Lengthwise Grain Measure from the top neck rim of the dress form at center back to waistline plus desired skirt length plus 2 inches.

   Crosswise Grain Measure across bust level (hip level if wider) from underarm seam to center back plus 5 inches.

2. Cut muslin thread perfect on the lengthwise and crosswise grains the amount measured.

3. Block muslin until grain perfect and press.

4. Identify grainlines.

   A. Measure in 1 inch from the cut lengthwise edge and identify the center back lengthwise grain in pencil.

   B. Fold under the 1-inch extension at center back and crease lightly with fingers.

   C. Place center back fold to center back of dress form with crosswise grains parallel to floor, pin center back at neckline, bust level, hip level and bottom of dress form torso. Crossmark neckline and waistline at center back. (**Figure 9-10**)

   D. Smooth and pin muslin crosswise grain straight across shoulder blade level taking and pinning ease (⅛ inch on double), mark at armplate.

   E. Pin muslin at hip level. Be sure crosswise grains are parallel to floor and ½ inch ease is included. Pin and crossmark back muslin directly over front underarm seam, at bust and hip level intersections. (**Figure 9-10**)

   F. Remove from dress form.

   G. Identify crosswise grain across muslin at the shoulder blade level (top one-quarter

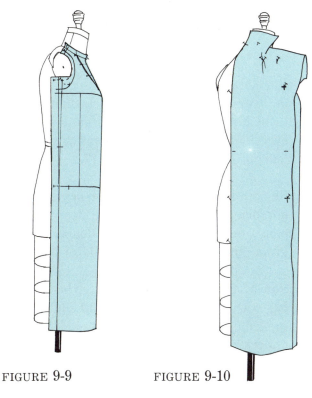

FIGURE 9-9   FIGURE 9-10

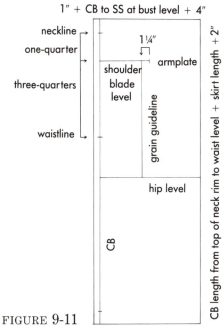

FIGURE 9-11

center-back length from neckline to waist level).

   H. Identify crosswise grain across muslin from crossmark at hip level underarm seam intersection. (**Figure 9-11**)

   I. At shoulder blade level identify lengthwise grain guideline to hip level, 1¼ inches in (toward center back) from armplate crossmark. (**Figure 9-11**)

99

Draping the Back Shift

1. Pin center back fold of muslin to center back of dress form at neckline, shoulder blade level, hip level and bottom of dress form torso aligning hip level crosswise grain with hip level of front shift. (**Figure 9-12**)

2. Smooth and pin crosswise grain across shoulder blade level parallel to the floor to armplate, taking ⅛ inch ease on double, before grain guideline. (**Figure 9-12**)

3. Smooth crosswise grain across hip level aligning with hip level of front shift and taking ¼ inch ease on double between guideline and underarm seam. Be sure hip level is parallel to floor and ease fold is directed diagonally from shoulder blade level to bottom edge of muslin inward toward center back. Pin hip level at underarm seam. (**Figures 9-12, 9-13**)

4. Pin muslin at armplate and underarm seam intersection, keeping grain guideline hanging at right angles from shoulder blade to hip levels.

   Note There should be considerable air space between grain guideline and dress form for comfort and flattering silhouette.

5. Smooth muslin across neckline and up to shoulder intersection, slash and pin as necessary. (**Figure 9-13**)

6. To determine ease and depth of shoulder dart drape muslin at shoulder blade level and armplate, up toward front shoulder and pin.

7. Smooth muslin across shoulder taking a pinch of ease midway between neckline and front shoulder dart and midway between armhole and front shoulder dart. Mark a vertical crossmark directly over front shoulder dart. (See **Figure 7-17, page 82.**)

8. To form back shoulder dart, fold on vertical crossmark and smooth excess fullness underneath. Pin dart at shoulder seam with dart

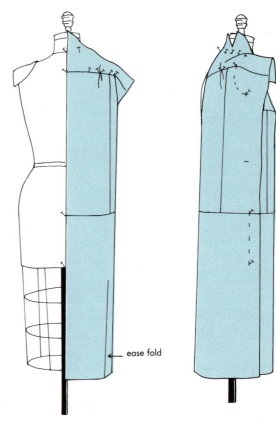

ease fold

FIGURE 9-12   FIGURE 9-13

depth folded inward toward center back. (See Figures 7-17, 7-18, page 83).

9. **Mark:**

   A. Neckline Mark along neckline and crossmark shoulder intersection.

   B. Shoulder Mark back shoulder; crossmark either side of and across shoulder dart. Crossmark armhole intersection. Place vertical mark at the princess seam of dress form 3 inches below back shoulder seam. Be sure the back shoulder seam marks follow the shoulder seam of the front shift. (See **Figure 7-17, page 83.**)

   C. Armhole Mark armplate underarm seam intersection and lowered armhole crossmark directly from front shift. Mark armplate from screw level to underarm seam. (**Figure 9-13**)

   D. Underarm Seam Mark directly from front shift, waistline crossmark and from hip level to bottom edge of dress form torso. (**Figure 9-13**)

Trueing the Back Shift

1. Remove back muslin from dress form.

2. Connect either side of shoulder dart to princess line mark to vanish 3 inches below shoulder seam.

3. Pin dart closed, true shoulder seam and neckline.

4. To true underarm seam, connect crossmarks from armplate to hip level in a straight line. At lowered armhole crossmark square a line out ½ inch from underarm seam and connect to underarm seam at hip level in a straight line. From hip level to bottom edge of muslin blend marks at side seam with a straight line. (**Figure 9-14**)

5. True armhole. Mark an armhole guideline with a broken line from armplate crossmark at shoulder blade level intersection 2 inches down lengthwise grain toward waistline.

6. Add seam allowances:

   A. ½ inch at neckline and armhole

   B. 1 inch at shoulder and underarm seam

   Cut excess muslin.

7. Remove muslin from dress form keeping shoulder dart pinned closed.

8. Pin back shoulder seam over front matching intersections. Pin underarm seam back over front, matching armhole, waistline and hip level.

9. Return shift muslin to dress form to check accuracy, fit and silhouette. (**Figures 9-15, 9-16, 9-17**) Be sure armhole is 1½ inches below plate, and there is ease (½ inch on double) extending beyond body line of the dress form to underarm seam. The shape of the armhole oval from the front, side and back views should be pleasing to the eye before pinning in the sleeve.

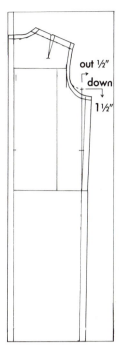

out ½"
down
1½"

FIGURE 9-14

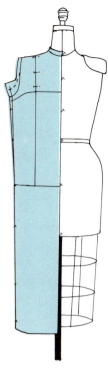

FIGURE 9-15

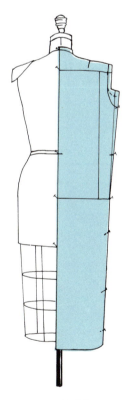

FIGURE 9-16

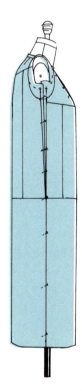

FIGURE 9-17

Preparing Muslin for the Sleeve

To draft set-in straight sleeve sloper, see **Drafting the Straight Sleeve Sloper, pages 104–107.** Transfer paper sleeve draft onto muslin.

1. Estimate yardage.

   Lengthwise Grain 2 inches plus length of sleeve at center.

   Crosswise Grain 3 inches plus width at biceps level.

2. Cut muslin thread perfect on the lengthwise and crosswise grains the amounts measured.

3. Block muslin until grain perfect and press.

4. Identify grainlines from sleeve draft to muslin in pencil. (**Figure 9-18**)

5. Transfer paper sleeve draft onto muslin matching grainlines. (**Figure 9-19**)

6. True the cap, sides and bottom of sleeve. (**Figure 9-18**)

7. Add seam allowances:

   A. ½ inch at sleeve cap and wrist

   B. 1 inch at sleeve underarm seam

8. Ease stitch the sleeve cap on the seamline from back to front underarm seam.

9. Pin sleeve underarm seams together, back over front, matching grain levels.

10. At top center of sleeve cap pick up a stitch from the bobbin thread side, forming a loop to gather ease for a capping effect from crossmark to crossmark. There is no ease below crossmarks. The sleeve cap should have just enough ease for a capping effect and a smooth armhole seam when stitched. There is no ease at the top curve of the sleeve cap for at least ½ inch on each side of the shoulder seam.

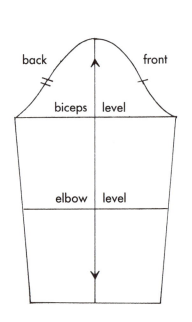

FIGURE 9-18

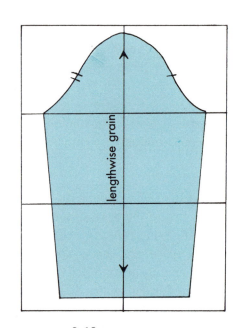

FIGURE 9-19

Pinning the Sleeve to the Shift

The center of the sleeve usually meets the shoulder seam of the shift. To determine the exact position, adjust the sleeve at the shoulder until the biceps level is parallel to the floor and the lengthwise grainline from shoulder to elbow hangs at a right angle. The lengthwise grain meets the side seam at wrist level. (**Figure 9-20**) (The sleeve will hang slightly forward toward the front when the lengthwise grain meets the side seam at wrist level.)

The sleeve underarm and biceps level intersection match the shift armhole/underarm seam intersection. With the sleeve hanging in this position:

1. Pin sleeve at shoulder, at crossmarks to front and back armhole and at underarm intersection. At crossmarks be sure to keep the cross-

wise grain across the sleeve cap parallel to the floor. (**Figures 9-21, 9-22**)

2. With the four main points established, fold under the sleeve seam allowance, lapping it over the armhole seam and begin a continuous line of vertical pins parallel to the edge. **Note:**

A. When the cap height of sleeve is longer than the armhole of the shift at the underarm seam, raise the biceps level at underarm seam reducing the cap height the amount needed to match intersection of shift underarm seam.

B. When the cap height of sleeve is shorter than the armhole of the shift at underarm seam, lower the biceps level at underarm seam, adding to the cap height the amount needed to match intersection of shift underarm seam.

FIGURE 9-20

FIGURE 9-21

FIGURE 9-22

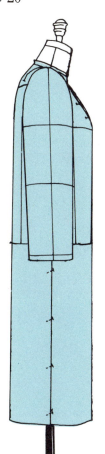

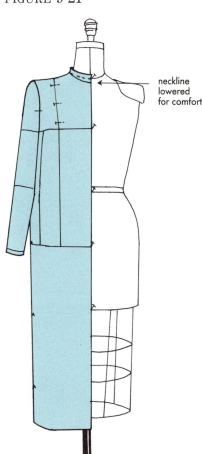

neckline lowered for comfort

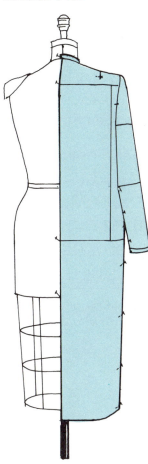

Drafting—developing a pattern from body measurements—is the most efficient method for developing the straight sleeve sloper. It does not concern itself with the design or position of darts and curves, but rather hinges on the problems of meticulous accuracy of shape. An endless variety of sleeve designs can be derived from this sloper.

The arm must be free to move in all directions, reaching, bending forward and upward.

The arm performs a great number of movements and a sleeve must have the adaptability to accommodate them. This makes the sleeve sloper one of the most complicated of all pattern shapes and requires absolute accuracy. Drafting is the most reliable method to provide the fit necessary for the arm in motion.

Note The straight sleeve sloper eliminates the elbow ease and therefore, cannot be used as a long fitted sleeve.

SLEEVE MEASUREMENTS* (in inches)

SIZES (women's)	14W	16W	18W	20W	22W	24W	26W
CAP HEIGHT	7¼	7⅜	7½	7⅝	7¾	7⅞	8
UNDERARM LENGTH	16½	16¾	17	17¼	17½	17¾	18
BICEPS CIRCUMFERENCE	16¾	17⅜	18	18⅝	19¼	19⅞	20½
ELBOW CIRCUMFERENCE	14¾	15⅜	16	16⅝	17¼	17⅞	18½
WRIST CIRCUMFERENCE	12¼	13	13¾	14½	15¼	16	16¾
SIZES (women's petite)	14WP	16WP	18WP	20WP	22WP	24WP	26WP
CAP HEIGHT	7	7⅛	7¼	7⅜	7½	7⅝	7¾
UNDERARM LENGTH	15⅜	15⅝	15⅞	16⅛	16⅜	16⅝	16⅞
BICEPS CIRCUMFERENCE	16¾	17⅜	18	18⅝	19¼	19⅞	20½
ELBOW CIRCUMFERENCE	14¾	15⅜	16	16⅝	17¼	17⅞	18½
WRIST CIRCUMFERENCE	12¼	13	13¾	14½	15¼	16	16¾

* Sleeve measurements include all ease allowed for a normal armhole and thin shoulder pads.

Figure 10-1

1. Size of paper—30″ × 24″.

2. Fold paper in half lengthwise. Place fold toward you.

3. Square a line from fold at top right of paper. This line represents the top of the *sleeve cap*.

4. From capline, measure down on fold of paper the depth of cap, this represents the *biceps level*. At this point, square a line from fold of paper one-half of biceps measurement and crossmark.

5. From biceps level, measure down on fold of paper one-half of underarm length minus ½ inch (the ½ inch is subtracted after the underarm measurement has been divided). At this point, square a line from fold of paper one-half of elbow measurement and crossmark.

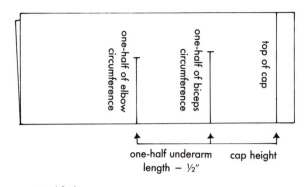

FIGURE 10-1

Figure 10-2

1. To establish underarm seam, connect biceps crossmark to elbow crossmark with a straight line, extending line to bottom of paper.

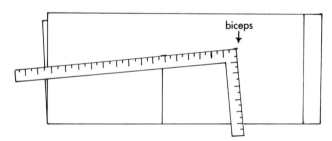

FIGURE 10-2

Figure 10-3

1. At underarm seam, measure down from biceps level underarm sleeve measurement and crossmark wrist point.

2. Square a line from fold of sleeve to wrist point. This represents the *wrist level*.

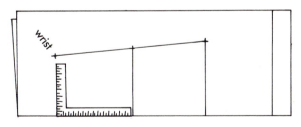

FIGURE 10-3

Figure 10-4

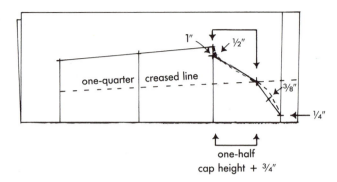

FIGURE 10-4

1. Crease sleeve in quarters by bringing center fold of sleeve to underarm seam.

2. To shape cap of sleeve, measure up from biceps level on crease line one-half of cap height plus ¾ inch. Crossmark.

3. Measure from underarm seam on biceps level 1 inch. Crossmark.

4. Connect the two crossmarks with a straight line.

5. Measure from center fold on cap line ¼ inch. Crossmark.

6. Connect with a straight line cap and crease line crossmarks. Curve armhole as illustrated with french curve.
   Note Armhole curve remains on biceps line for ¼ inch at underarm intersection.

7. With paper folded, trace through underarm seam.

8. With paper folded, cut through on armhole, wrist, and underarm seamlines.

Figure 10-5

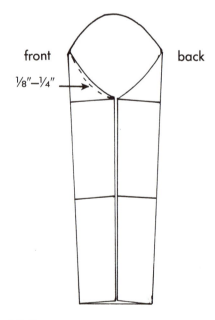

FIGURE 10-5

1. Open sleeve pattern. Continue biceps and elbow levels across pattern. Be sure they are at right angles to center fold.

2. Pencil in center line over crease. Identify center line as the *lengthwise grain*.

3. Fold sleeve in quarters by bringing underarm seam of sleeve to meet at center of sleeve (see illustration).

4. **Front armhole** For proper fit, this type of armhole needs to be scooped at front ⅛ to ¼ inch as illustrated.

Figure 10-6

Fold cap of sleeve in half by bringing top of cap to biceps level.

A. Front Crossmark fold at armhole line.

B. Back Crossmark fold at armhole line and another crossmark ½ inch below.

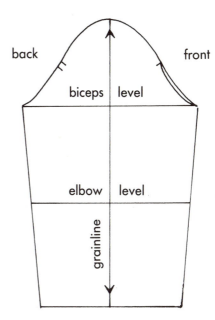

FIGURE 10-6

Figure 10-7

1. If some elbow ease is desired, cut center of sleeve (lengthwise grain) from wrist to elbow level and on elbow level from underarm seam to center of sleeve. Overlap draft at wrist and spread elbow ½ inch.

2. Establish crossmarks for control of ease as illustrated.

3. To establish new lengthwise grain, continue upper sleeve grainline to wrist (center of sleeve will no longer be on grain).

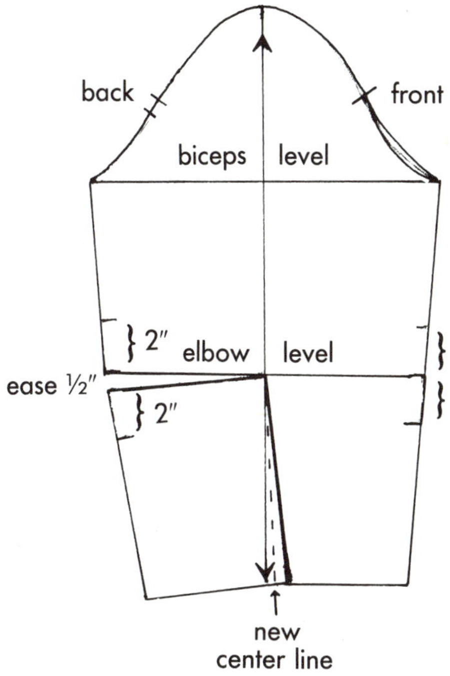

FIGURE 10-7

Converting Dress Sleeve Sloper to Suit Sleeve Sloper

When a good dress sleeve sloper has been developed, it may be used as the foundation pattern for a suit sleeve sloper. The sleeve will fit with the same precision as the original drafted master sleeve pattern.

A two-piece set-in sleeve, because it is made in two sections, fits more exactly than the one piece. It is used for tailored garments and can be used as a foundation pattern from which to design variations of two-piece straight or shaped suit sleeves.

The illustrations on the following pages show at a glance the step by step development for converting a one- and two-piece straight and shaped suit sleeve.

107

Straight Dress Sleeve to One-Piece Suit Sleeve

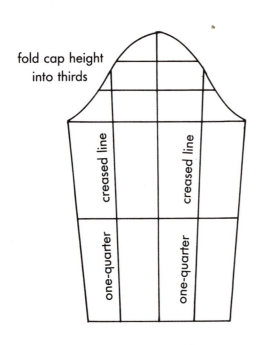

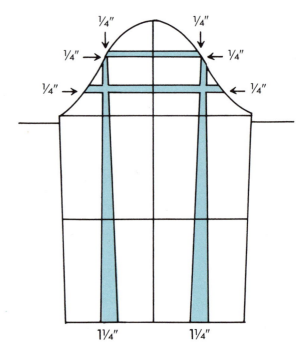

FIGURE 10-8   **Dress Sleeve Sloper**   FIGURE 10-9   **Straight Suit Sleeve Sloper**

Two-Piece Straight Suit Sleeve Sloper

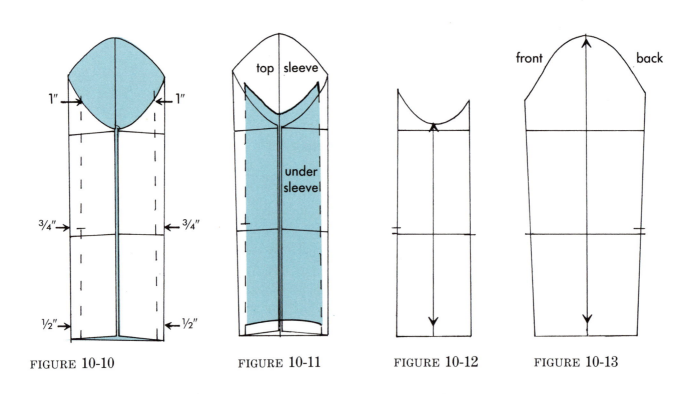

FIGURE 10-10   FIGURE 10-11   FIGURE 10-12   FIGURE 10-13

One-Piece Suit Sleeve with Elbow Ease

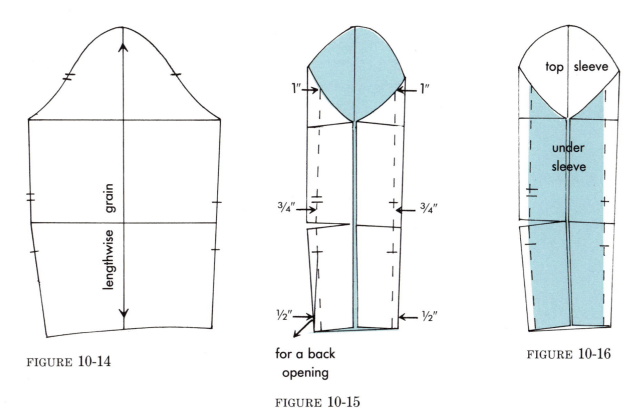

FIGURE 10-14

for a back
opening

FIGURE 10-15

FIGURE 10-16

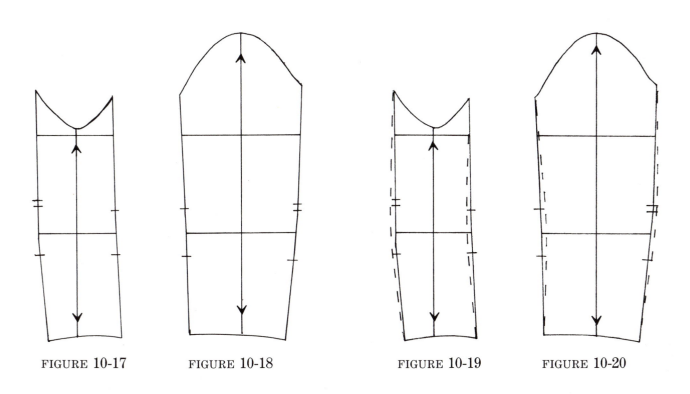

FIGURE 10-17 FIGURE 10-18 FIGURE 10-19 FIGURE 10-20

If more shape is desired, seamlines may be
curved (broken line).

The torso jacket sloper is molded to fit the figure extending to or below the hip level without a waistline seam. It may be fitted snugly, close to the figure at the waistline or loosely, away from the figure at the waistline to accommodate the prevailing silhouette. The torso jacket sloper is draped with additional ease for comfort. Shoulder pads are an asset to the plus-size figure, and should be pinned to the dress form before draping begins.

Preparing Muslin for the Front Torso Jacket

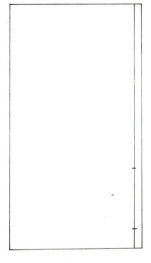

FIGURE 11-1

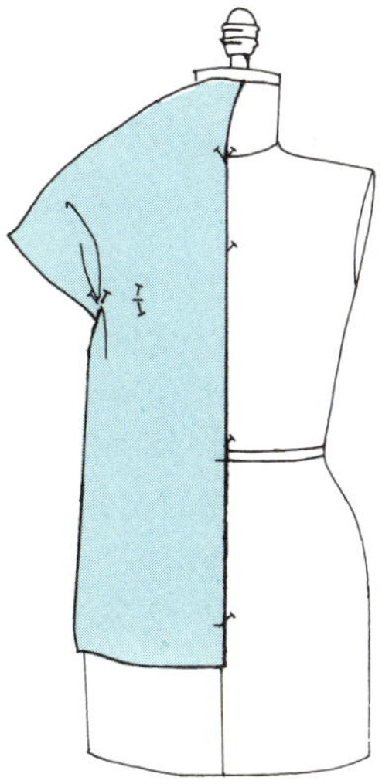

FIGURE 11-2

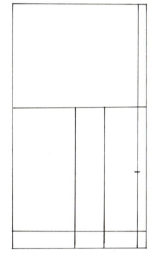

FIGURE 11-3

1. Estimate yardage. (**Figure 11-1**)
   Lengthwise Grain Measure from the top neck rim of the dress form to waistline plus 10 inches.
   Crosswise Grain Measure across bust level from underarm seam to center front plus 6 inches.

2. Cut muslin thread perfect.

3. Block and press muslin.

4. Identify grainlines.

   A. Measure in 1 inch from the cut lengthwise edge and identify center front lengthwise grains. (**Figure 11-1**)

   B. Measure up from bottom crosswise grain 2 inches, crossmark hip level. (**Figure 11-1**)

   C. Measure up from bottom crosswise grain 10 inches and crossmark center front at waist level. (**Figure 11-1**)

   D. Fold under the 1-inch extension at center front and crease lightly with fingers.

   E. Pin waist level crossmark at center front fold to center front of dress form at bottom of waistline tape. Keeping crosswise grains parallel to floor, pin center front fold to dress form above and below bust level, at neck and hip level.

   F. Drape muslin so that crosswise grain is straight across bust level from center front, pin at apex and underarm seam taking and pinning ease ¼ inch on double between apex and underarm seam. Crossmark apex and bust level, mark underarm seam at bust level. (**Figure 11-2**)

   G. Remove muslin from dress form.

   H. Identify crosswise grain at bust level from apex to center front and across full width of muslin. (**Figure 11-3**)

   I. Identify crosswise grain from bust level to bottom edge of muslin at apex and halfway from apex to underarm seam (these grain guidelines will become the center of darts). (**Figure 11-3**)

111

Draping the Front Torso Jacket

1. Place center front fold of muslin to center front of dress form with crosswise grain parallel to floor at bust level. Pin at apex, smooth muslin across chest and toward neckline, pin center front at neckline, between neckline and bust level and between bust level and waistline. (**Figure 11-4**)

2. Maintaining crosswise grain parallel to floor, continue to pin center front fold at waistline and hip level and in between. (**Figure 11-4**)

3. Drape muslin so that crosswise grain at bust level is straight across (parallel to floor) and the lengthwise grains below bust level hang like a box at right angles to crosswise grain. Pin bust level between apex and underarm seam taking and pinning ease ¼ inch on double, pin at underarm seam. (**Figure 11-4**)

4. Smooth muslin at neckline, keeping grains at right angles to each other. Pin neckline midway between center front and shoulder. Slash muslin diagonally from top edge of muslin at center front to midway pin stopping ½ inch above neckline seam of dress form. (**Figure 11-5**)

5. To keep the depth of neck dart as narrow as possible, at armhole and shoulder intersection, hold edge of muslin upward and smooth down over shoulder, coaxing as much ease as possible into hollow area from apex to armhole above bust level, and still maintain a smooth armhole seam.
   Note There will be considerable air space between the muslin and dress form. The armhole seam area should appear smooth with close to the body fit.

6. Smooth muslin at shoulder seam, directing excess to neck, pin at shoulder and armhole intersection and shoulder and neckline intersection. (**Figure 11-5**)

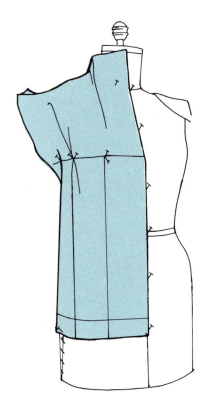

FIGURE 11-4

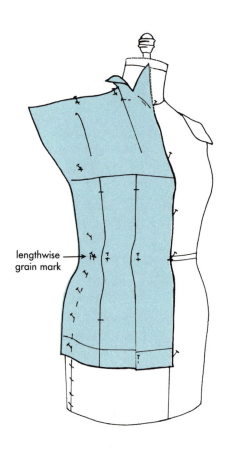

lengthwise grain mark

FIGURE 11-5

7. To drape neck dart, smooth excess muslin toward midway point at neck and position dart parallel to center front to its vanishing point at approximately one-third the front neckline measurement from shoulder and neckline intersection. Pin dart at neck with its under depth folded inward toward center front. (**Figure 11-5**)

   Note The objective is to coax the neck dart as close to the center front as possible (without any diagonal pulls) so it can be easily concealed by lapels, collars, and design details.

8. To determine depth of torso darts and underarm seam, lightly crease muslin on dart grain guidelines.

9. At underarm/armplate intersection, follow lengthwise grain down to waistline and mark lightly in pencil at waistline. (**Figure 11-5**)

10. Mold muslin to dress form at waist level to desired silhouette fit, pinning darts at waistline vertically with the center of darts, the creased fold, extending outward (dart depth approximately ½ inch or less on double depending on snugness desired). (**Figure 11-5**)

11. Mold underarm seam to dress form in toward center front approximately ½ inch or less from lengthwise grain at waistline. (**Figure 11-5**)

    Note A snug-fitting silhouette, to be comfortable, requires ¼-inch ease at waistline from underarm seam to center front.

12. To complete the shaping of darts to hip level, pin apex dart vertically at hip level ⅛ inch on double with the creased fold extending outward. (**Figure 11-5**)

13. Dart closest to underarm seam is shorter below waist level and will vanish above hip level at the high hip bone.

14. Pin underarm seam to hip level allowing ½ inch ease from underarm seam to center front.

FIGURE 11-6

15. **Mark: (Figures 11-5, 11-6)**

    A. **Neckline** Crossmark neckline at center front intersection and along neckline at 1-inch intervals and across pinned dart to shoulder.

    B. **Neck Dart** Mark either side of dart from neckline to vanishing point. Crossmark vanishing point.

    C. **Shoulder** Crossmark shoulder and neckline intersection and shoulder and armhole intersection.

    D. **Armhole** Mark the armhole ridge from shoulder to just above the armplate screw level. Crossmark intersection of armplate and underarm seam; mark armplate to screw level at short intervals.

    E. **Underarm Seam** Crossmark intersection at armplate and underarm seam and intersection at underarm seam and bottom of waistline tape. Mark to hip level at short intervals.

    F. **Waist Torso Darts** Crossmark vanishing point at top of darts. Crossmark darts at waistline intersections (bottom of tape) and either side of dart depth. Mark either side of apex dart at hip level intersection. Crossmark vanishing point of shorter dart.

    G. Crossmark center front at waistline (bottom of tape).

113

Trueing the Front Torso Jacket

1. Remove muslin from dress form. Be sure all essential marks are on muslin. (**Figure 11-7**)

2. True neck dart by connecting crossmark nearest center front to vanishing point with a straight ruler. True dart side nearest shoulder by blending marks with hip curve from neckline to vanishing point. (**Figure 11-8**)

3. True torso waistline darts above waist level with straight ruler from vanishing point to crossmarks on either side of center grainline. The hip curve is used to complete darts on hip section of torso.

4. To true apex dart, place hip curve with straight, narrow end toward waistline with the approximate area of number 11 at hip level. Reverse hip curve to true other side of dart in the exact position. (**Figure 11-8**)

5. True either side of shorter torso dart with hip curve positioned to blend dartline from waistline to vanishing point. (**Figure 11-8**)

6. To true neckline seam, pin neck dart closed beginning at vanishing point with its under depth folded inward toward center front. At center front and neckline intersection, pencil crosswise grain across neckline ¼ inch. Blend neckline marks from ¼ inch crosswise grain across pinned dart to shoulder with french curve. (**Figure 11-8**)

7. To true shoulder seam, connect crossmarks at neckline and armhole ridge with a straight line.

FIGURE 11-7

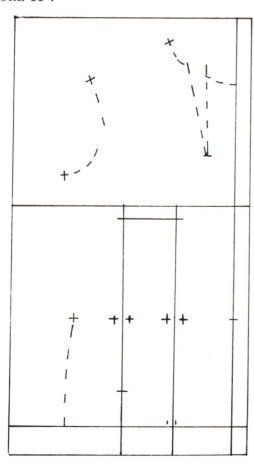

FIGURE 11-8

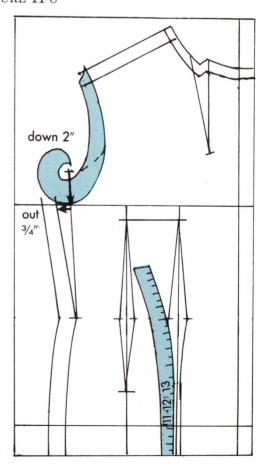

8. True underarm seam by connecting cross-marks at armplate and waistline with a straight line and blending marks from waistline to bottom edge with the hip curve. (**Figure 11-8**)

9. At underarm seam, lower armhole 2 inches from armplate, crossmark. At crossmark square a line out from underarm seam ¾ inch and connect to waistline with a straight ruler. (**Figure 11-8**)

   Note To allow ease needed for a set-in sleeve in a torso jacket, the armhole is lowered an additional ½ inch and extended an additional ¼ inch at the underarm seam than the bodice sloper.

10. To true armhole, position french curve so that the deepest curve touches the lowered 2-inch level of the armhole, and the outside edge aligns with shoulder and armhole ridge marks or falls between the marks at the plate screw level. (**Figure 11-8**)

11. Add ½ inch seam allowance at neckline, 1 inch at shoulder and underarm seamline.

Preparing Muslin for the Back Torso Jacket

1. Estimate yardage.

   Lengthwise Grain Measure from the center back top to neck rim of the dress form to waistline plus 10 inches.

   Crosswise Grain Measure across back at bust level from underarm seam to center back plus 6 inches.

2. Cut muslin thread perfect.

3. Block and press muslin.

4. Identify grainlines.

   A. Pin back to front muslin making sure that the back lengthwise and crosswise grain edges meet the lengthwise and crosswise grain edges of the front torso at the underarm and bottom edges as illustrated. (**Figure 11-9**)

   B. Using colored tracing paper, carbon side up, place muslin back and front pinned together, with back over carbon. Front torso pattern will be facing up.

   C. With tracing wheel, trace front body line and extended underarm seam and seam allowance to the back. (**Figure 11-10**)

   D. At underarm seam trace crossmark at armplate and waistline. (**Figure 11-10**)

   E. Crossmark with tracing wheel bust level and hip level at underarm lengthwise edge. (**Figure 11-10**)

   F. Remove tracing paper. Keep back and front pinned together along lengthwise edge.

5. Vertical pin underarm seam at armplate, waist level and hip level crossmarks.

6. Cut excess muslin from front neckline and shoulder seam. Cut front armhole roughly, leaving 2½ inches above armhole at under-

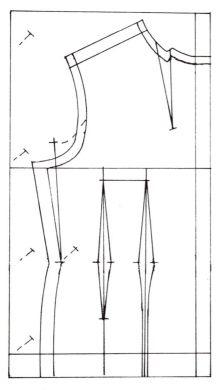

FIGURE 11-9

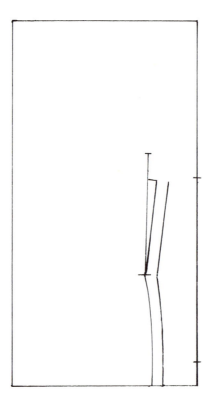

FIGURE 11-10

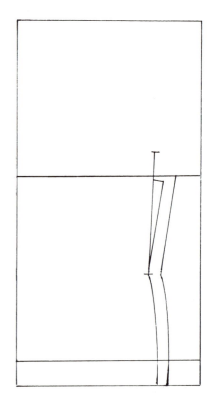

FIGURE 11-11

116

arm seam intersection and 1 inch to shoulder seam. Do not cut excess muslin at underarm seam. (**Figure 11-12**)

7. Pin front torso darts closed. Crease lightly dartlines nearest center front and bring the creased line to meet other side of dart beginning at waistline and ending at vanishing points above waistline. (**Figure 11-12**)

8. Pin apex dart below waistline down to bottom edge, matching grains at hip level. (**Figure 11-12**)

9. Pin shorter dart from waistline to vanishing point. (**Figure 11-12**)

10. Return front torso to dress form being careful that all marks are accurately pinned. At shoulder seam, sink pins completely into dress form so that seam allowance is held flat and molded to dress form.

11. Pin body line of underarm seam securely to dress form at armplate, at waist and hip levels with excess muslin extending outward and pinned to back muslin.

Draping the Back Torso Jacket

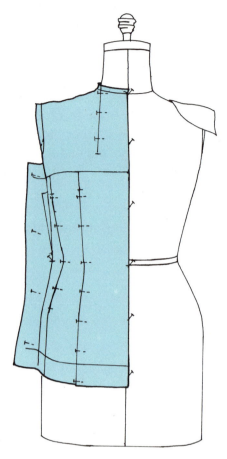

1. Pin back body line of underarm seam securely to dress form at armplate and at waist and hip levels. (**Figure 11-13**)

2. With muslin secured to back underarm seam of dress form, hold top edge of muslin and smooth up at armhole to shoulder blade level, pin and crossmark at armplate. (**Figure 11-13**)
   Note There should be air space between muslin and dress form below shoulder blade and above bust levels in armplate area. The armhole should have a smooth, close to the body fit.

3. Pin crosswise grain parallel to floor across shoulder blade to center back, taking and pinning ¼ inch ease on double, 1¼ inches from armplate. (**Figure 11-13**)

FIGURE 11-12

4. Crossmark center back at shoulder blade area. With pin, follow lengthwise grain to bottom edge of muslin. (**Figure 11-13**)

5. At center back crossmark waistline at bottom of tape. Smooth muslin to neckline and crossmark. (**Figure 11-13**)

6. Remove muslin from dress form keeping front and back pinned together at underarm.

7. Identify lengthwise grain at center back from mark at shoulder blade area to top and bottom edge of muslin. (**Figure 11-13**)

8. Add 1-inch seam allowance at center back. Cut excess muslin. (**Figure 11-13**)

9. Fold center back length from neckline to waistline crossmarks in quarters. Top one-quarter of center back length equals shoulder blade level. Identify crosswise grain across shoulder blade level in pencil. (**Figure 11-14**)

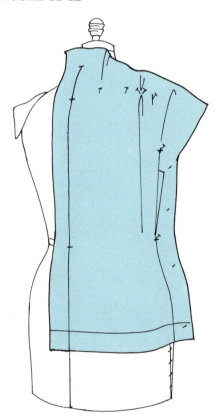

FIGURE 11-13

The crosswise grainline at bust level has been purposely eliminated to present a clearer illustration.

118

10. Identify in pencil crosswise grain at bust and hip levels from traced crossmarks at edge of muslin to center back. (**Figure 11-14**)

11. With back and front torso pinned together at underarm seam, cut excess muslin at 1-inch seam allowance to top edge. Unpin back and front torso.

12. Pin underarm seam back over front, matching crossmarks at 2-inch lowered armhole, at waist and hip levels. Pin in between. To avoid diagonal pulls, slash seam allowance at waistline, stopping short of seamline.

13. With underarm seam pinned together, vertical pin body line at lowered armhole intersection.

14. From center back waist level, mark the same distance of front apex torso dart to center front, with a vertical crossmark at waistline. (**Figure 11-14**)

15. Return front and back torso to dress form being careful that all marks are accurately pinned. At front shoulder seam, sink pins completely into dress form so that seam allowance is held flat and molded to dress form.

16. Pin body line of underarm seam securely to dress form at armplate, waist and hip levels. (**Figures 11-15, 11-16**)

17. Fold under 1-inch extension at center back, crease lightly. Pin to dress form accurately at neckline, shoulder blade level and waistline. (**Figure 11-14**)

18. Pin shoulder blade level across to armplate parallel to floor taking and pinning ¼ inch ease on double. (**Figure 11-14**)

19. To determine depth of torso darts, mold muslin to desired silhouette fit at waistline to accommodate two darts of equal depth (approximately ½ inch or less on double), with the dart nearest center back pinned

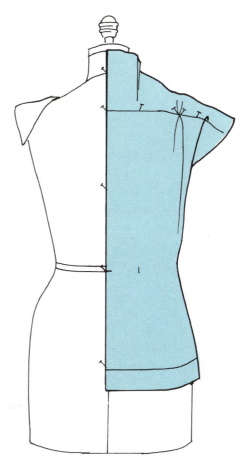

FIGURE 11-14

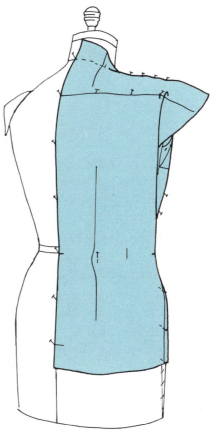

FIGURE 11-15

vertically at waistline crossmark, and center of dart fold extending outward. Mark either side of dart at waistline. (**Figure 11-15**)

20. Release pin of second dart. Measure and mark one-half the distance from pinned dart to underarm seam with a vertical crossmark at waistline. (**Figure 11-15**)

21. Follow lengthwise grain at vertical crossmark to bottom edge of muslin with pin.

22. Vertical pin depth of second dart at waistline with center of dart fold extending outward. (**Figure 11-16**)

23. To complete shaping of darts to hip level, follow lengthwise grain of dart fold nearest center back to bottom edge of muslin. Pin dart at hip level ⅛ inch on double with center of dart fold extending outward. Mark either side of dart at hip level. (**Figure 11-16**)

24. Crossmark vanishing point of second dart below waistline at center of dart fold. (**Figure 11-16**)

Note Second dart of back will be longer than dart at front.

There should be ½ inch ease from underarm seam across hip level to center back.

25. Crossmark vanishing points of torso darts above waistline. (**Figure 11-16**)

26. Mark armplate from underarm intersection to armplate screw level. (**Figure 11-16**)

27. Smooth muslin at neckline, keeping grains at right angles to each other. Pin neckline midpoint from center back to shoulder seam. Slash from top edge of muslin toward neckline, stopping ½ inch above neckline seam. (**Figure 11-17**)

28. Smooth muslin up to shoulder from shoulder blade level at armplate crossmark, pin shoulder and armhole intersection. (**Figure 11-17**)

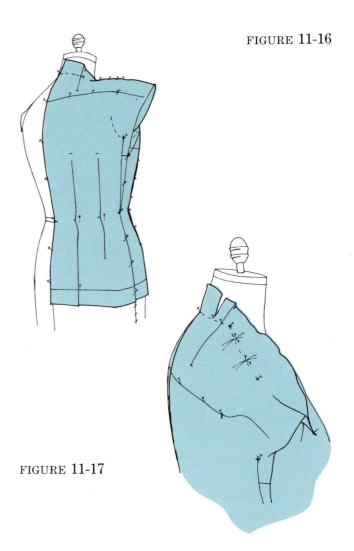

FIGURE 11-16

FIGURE 11-17

29. Smooth muslin across shoulder taking and pinning a pinch of ease on either side of center. Pin shoulder and neckline intersection. (**Figure 11-17**)

30. To determine neckline dart, smooth excess muslin toward pin at shoulder. Neckline dart is centered on dress form from pin at midway slash and shoulder. Crossmark muslin at this point. Crease crossmark, smooth excess muslin underneath and pin dart with its under depth folded inward toward center back. (**Figure 11-17**)

31. Mark neckline from center back across and either side of neckline dart to shoulder at inch intervals. Crossmark either side of dart. (**Figure 11-17**)

32. Mark shoulder seam directly over front shoulder seam at inch intervals and at neckline/armhole intersections. (**Figure 11-17**)

Trueing the Back Torso Jacket

1. Remove muslin from dress form keeping back and front pinned together at underarm seam. (**Figure 11-18**)

2. To true back torso darts, identify lengthwise grain in pencil at center of darts from vanishing points above waistline to bottom edge of muslin. (**Figure 11-19**)

3. True both darts above waistline with a straight ruler from vanishing point to either side of dart depth at waistline crossmarks. The hip curve is used to complete darts on hip section of torso. True dart nearest center back, place hip curve with straight narrow end toward waistline as in instructions for **Trueing the Front Torso Jacket, #4 and #5.** (**Figure 11-19**)

4. Using straight ruler, connect crossmark of neck dart nearest center back to vanishing point of waistline dart nearest the center back. Measure down from neckline 3 inches and crossmark vanishing point of neck dart. Connect opposite side of neck dart to vanishing point. (**Figure 11-19**)

5. To true neckline seam, pin neck dart closed, beginning at vanishing point with its under depth folded inward toward center back. At center back and neckline intersection, pencil crosswise grain ¼ to ½ inch. Blend neckline marks from one-quarter to one-half of crosswise grain across pinned dart to shoulder, using french curve. (**Figure 11-19**)

6. To true shoulder, position hip curve and blend a shallow curve from shoulder and neckline intersection to center of shoulder and a nearly straight line to armhole intersection.

7. True armhole.

   A. With straight ruler, draw a broken armhole guideline from armplate crossmark at shoulder blade level to waistline and underarm seam intersection. (**Figure 11-19**)

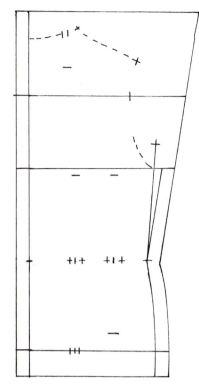

FIGURE 11-18

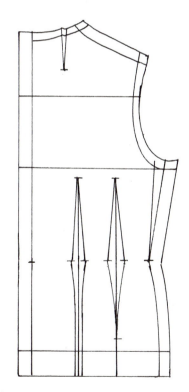

FIGURE 11-19

B. Position french curve against guideline for approximately 2 inches from arm-plate crossmark at shoulder blade level, with deepest outside curve touching the lowered armhole crossmark, the outside straighter edge aligns with shoulder and armhole intersection. True armhole line with french curve held steady in this position. (**Figure 11-19**)

8. Add ½ inch seam allowance to neckline seam with dart pinned closed, and 1 inch to shoulder. Cut excess muslin.

9. Add ½ inch seam allowance to front and back armhole seam. Cut excess muslin.

10. Pin back torso darts closed. Crease lightly dartlines nearest center back and bring creased line to meet other side of darts beginning at waistline and ending at vanishing points above waistline. Complete pinning dart nearest center back matching grains at hip level. Pin shorter dart to vanishing point above hip level. Darts are pinned with their under depth folded inward toward center back. Slash back and front dart under depths at waistline stopping short of seamline.

11. Pin shoulder seams together, back over front matching neckline and armhole intersections. Distribute ease evenly between matching intersections.

12. Return torso jacket to dress form for final checking. Pin center front at neckline above and below bust level, at waistline and at hip level. Pin center back at neckline, waistline, hip level and in between. Check the general effect and appearance of the entire torso jacket from all angles. Be sure the armhole is lowered from armplate 2 inches and there is ¾-inch ease on double extending beyond body line of the dress form to underarm seam. The shape of the armhole oval from all angles should be pleasing to the eye before pinning in the sleeve. (**Figures 11-20, 11-21**)

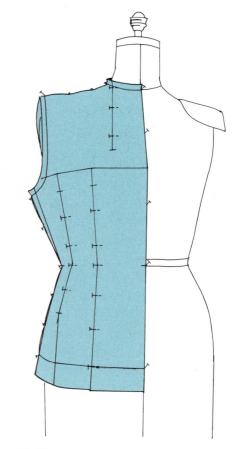

FIGURE 11-20

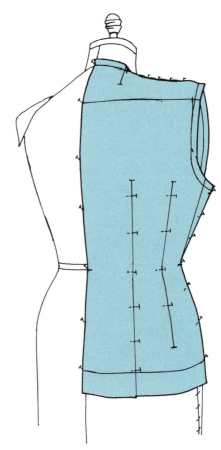

FIGURE 11-21

Preparing Muslin for the Straight Suit Sleeve

1. Follow instructions for **Converting Dress Sleeve Sloper to Suit Sleeve, pages 107–109.**

2. Follow instructions for **Preparing Muslin Sleeve, page 102.**

Pinning the Straight Suit Sleeve to the Fitted Torso Jacket

1. Follow directions **page 103.**

2. Crossmark torso front and back armhole at sleeve cap crossmarks. (**Figure 11-22**)

3. Be sure the crosswise grains of the sleeve at biceps level are parallel to floor and sleeve hangs slightly forward at wrist. (**Figures 11-22, 11-23**)

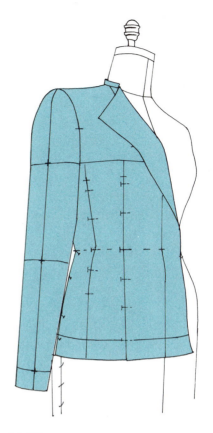

FIGURE 11-22

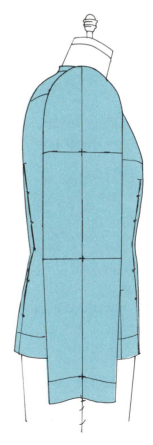

FIGURE 11-23

123

The raglan sleeve extends to the neckline. It has a smooth rounded shoulder, cut in one with the sleeve, and is set in by diagonal seams from the underarm to the front and back neckline. The raglan uses a shoulder seam dart to shape and fit the shoulder.

The raglan sleeve is distinguished from the kimono and dolman because it retains its original lower armhole line; the kimono and dolman by comparison lose the lower armhole curve when the sleeve is blended with the bodice.

In reality, the raglan sleeve is a variation of the set-in sleeve. Because it retains the lower armhole curve of a set-in sleeve, it fits the underarm more exactly. When the depth of the armhole is normal, the raglan falls in the same manner as any set-in sleeve. Often additional ease is added at the underarm, making it especially comfortable to wear and extensively used in tailored garments.

1. On the dress form identify desired front and back raglan seamline with style tape. Place style tape 1 inch below armplate screw level from armplate to neckline. (**Figure 12-1**) **Note** Style tape may be pinned directly to a completed bodice pattern. (**Figures 12-2, 12-3, 12-4**)

2. Estimate yardage. (**Figure 12-5**)

   Lengthwise Grain Measure 10 inches plus length of sleeve sloper plus 1 inch.

   Crosswise Grain Measure width across biceps level of sleeve sloper plus 6 inches.

3. Cut muslin thread perfect.

4. Block and press muslin.

5. Identify grainlines. (**Figure 12-5**)

   A. Lengthwise grain at center of muslin.

   B. To add additional ease for comfort, mark lengthwise grain ½ inch on each side of center grainline.

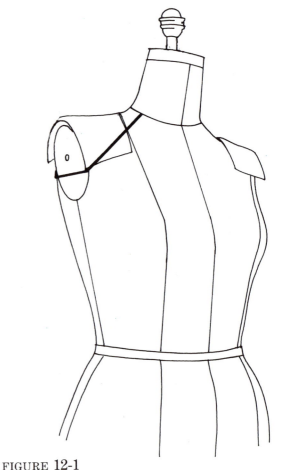

FIGURE 12-1

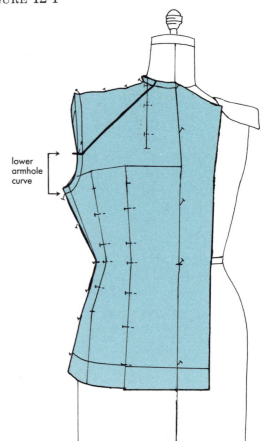

lower armhole curve

FIGURE 12-2

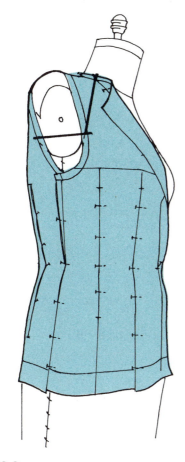

FIGURE 12-3

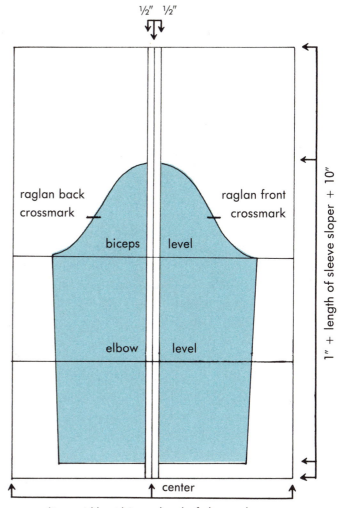

½″ ½″

raglan back
crossmark

raglan front
crossmark

biceps   level

elbow   level

center

1″ + length of sleeve sloper + 10″

6″ + width at biceps level of sleeve sloper

FIGURE 12-5

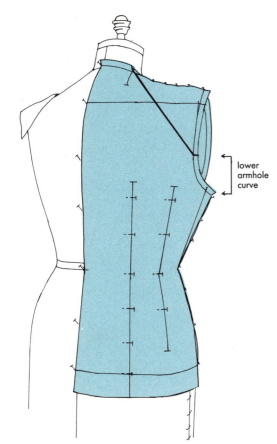

lower
armhole
curve

FIGURE 12-4

C. Crosswise grain at biceps level 10 inches plus height of cap from top edge of muslin.

D. Crosswise grain at elbow level.

6. Crossmark the cap of the sleeve sloper front and back (**Figure 12-6**), the exact measurement from underarm seam intersection at the bodice armhole front and back, from underarm seam intersection to crossmark at the taped raglan diagonal seam. (**Figures 12-2, 12-4**)

125

7. Copy the sleeve sloper below elbow level on prepared muslin. Lightly copy the sleeve cap above biceps level. Crossmark underarm seam at biceps level. Be sure to copy raglan seam crossmarks, front and back. (**Figure 12-7**)

8. Measure up ⅝ inch from biceps level underarm seam crossmarks. Identify crosswise grain out to edge of muslin, front and back. (**Figure 12-7**)

9. Measure out ¼ inch from raglan seam crossmark, front and back. (**Figure 12-7**)

10. At top center of sleeve cap, measure down 1 inch and crossmark across additional ease. (**Figure 12-7**)

11. Place front sleeve sloper on muslin, matching sloper raglan crossmark and the ¼ inch point on muslin. Utilizing the raglan seam crossmark of the sleeve cap as pivot point, pivot the underarm seam of the sleeve sloper up to the raised ⅝ inch biceps level. Holding the sleeve in this position, trace the lower cap of the sleeve onto muslin from raglan seam crossmark to underarm seam. Crossmark intersection. (**Figure 12-4**) Repeat for back.

12. To true underarm seams above the elbow level, connect at the raised biceps level to the underarm seam at elbow level with the hip curve. (**Figure 12-8**)

13. Add ½ inch seam allowance to the lower cap and wrist level. Add 1 inch seam allowance at underarm seams. Cut excess muslin as illustrated. (**Figure 12-9**)

14. Pin underarm seams of sleeve together back over front matching biceps, elbow and wrist levels.

15. Pin the lower cap of the sleeve front and back to the armhole of the bodice matching underarm seams and raglan seam crossmarks. (**Figure 12-10**)

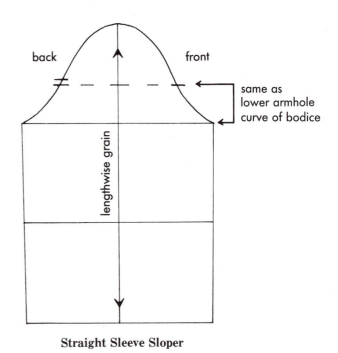

Straight Sleeve Sloper

FIGURE 12-6

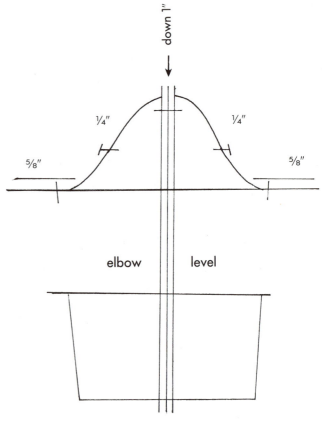

FIGURE 12-7

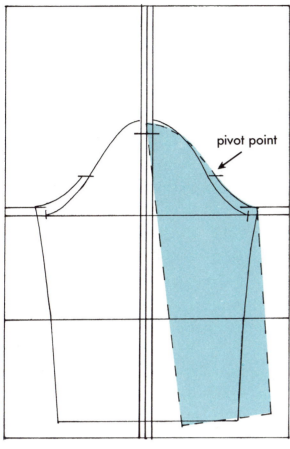

FIGURE 12-8

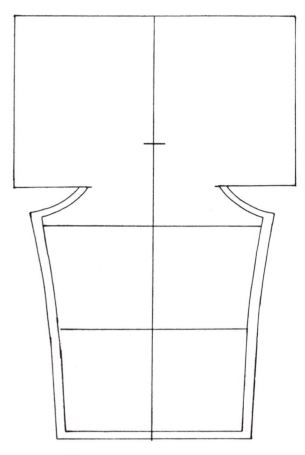

FIGURE 12-9

16. Hold the sleeve out at the center grainline so that if forms a 45° angle. Aim the 1-inch crossmark at top center of sleeve cap to shoulder/armhole intersection, smooth and pin muslin of front cap over bodice taped raglan seam to the neckline. (**Figure 12-10**) Repeat for back.

17. Smooth front and back excess muslin up to shoulder seam. Pin along shoulder seam from neckline to armhole intersection. Add ⅜-inch ease (depending on thickness of fabric) at shoulder and armhole ridge; blend shoulder seam from ease point to neckline. (**Figure 12-11**)

18. Blend shoulder seam forming dart from ease point to the center of the sleeve grainline, vanishing at approximately mid-level of cap height or above. (**Figure 12-11**)

19. Mark the sleeve at the taped raglan seam to neckline and crossmark neckline intersection front and back. (**Figure 12-11**)

20. Mark raglan sleeve neckline front and back.

21. Pencil mark shoulder seam along pins; crossmark shoulder seam dart at vanishing point, armhole ridge and neckline intersections.

22. Remove raglan sleeve from dress form keeping shoulder seams pinned together.

23. With shoulder seams pinned together, true the front shoulder, blending marks. Trace front shoulder to back using tracing wheel and carbon paper.

24. True front and back raglan seam.

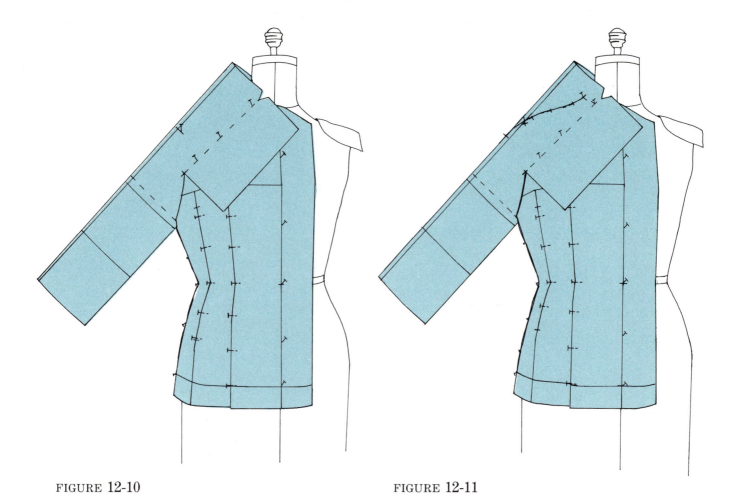

FIGURE 12-10

FIGURE 12-11

FIGURE 12-12

25. Add ½ inch seam allowance at raglan seam, front and back and 1 inch seam allowance at shoulder dart seams as illustrated. Cut excess muslin. (**Figure 12-12**)

   Note The raglan sleeve may be cut in two from vanishing point of shoulder seam dart along the center grainline to wrist. When this is done, seam allowance is added to each side of center grainline.

26. Mark torso jacket at taped raglan seam from crossmark to neckline front and back.

27. Remove front and back torso jacket from dress form keeping them pinned together.

28. *Remove* pins from shoulder seam *only*. True front and back raglan seam from lower armhole crossmark to neckline. Add ½ inch seam allowance. (**Figures 12-13, 12-14**)

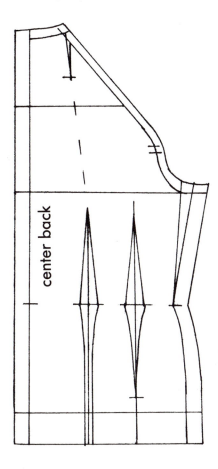

center back

FIGURE 12-13

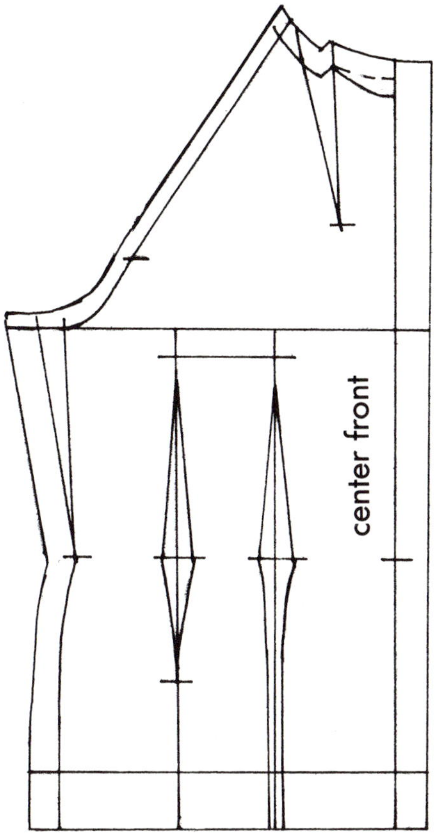

center front

FIGURE 12-14

29. Pin raglan sleeve at shoulder dart seams together, back over front matching crossmarks and neckline intersection.

30. Pin raglan sleeve underarm seams together.

31. Pin the raglan seams of the sleeve over the raglan seams of the front and back bodice matching raglan seam crossmarks and neckline intersection.

32. Pin the lower cap of raglan sleeve to lower armhole of bodice matching underarm seams.

33. True the raglan sleeve neckline blending marks to front and back bodice neckline. Add ½ inch seam allowance to neckline of raglan sleeve. Cut excess muslin.

34. Return muslin to dress form and check fit and appearance from all angles.

Pants have become one of the most popular fashion items worn for all occasions, ranging from a backyard barbeque to a white tie ball. They come in all lengths and widths, full and flowing, straight and tailored, tapered or flared, elegant or casual. Smart-looking pants outfits can be part of every woman's wardrobe, including the plus size.

The fit of pants for plus-size women is probably even more important than the fit of other garments, since pants outline the figure more. Pants for the plus-size customer must not only cover the body but must enhance their appearance as well. It is therefore very important that a basic pants sloper is draped with expert care to produce pants that are comfortable and fit well. A pants form is essential for draping pants slopers (**Figure 13-1**).

Pants for the full-figured customer should have fully or partially elasticized waists. The straight leg styles are best for all figure types. Slightly tapered legs are acceptable for those who have well-shaped legs that are in proportion with the hips.

Determine the crotch level. The crotch level becomes a level of control along with the waist and hip levels.

To determine the length of the crotch level, place the L-square between the legs of a pants form holding inner edges against the pants form at center front to the highest possible level. The length of the crotch level is the measurement that appears on the L-square at waist level (the bottom edge of the waistline tape) plus 1¼ inches ease (**Figure 13-2**).

The crotch ease may be increased for loose-fitting pants and decreased for close-fitting pants.

Preparing Muslin for the Front & Back Pants

1. Estimate yardage. (**Figure 13-3**)

   Lengthwise Grain Measure the desired length of pants plus 4 inches.

   Crosswise Grain Width of muslin from selvage to selvage.

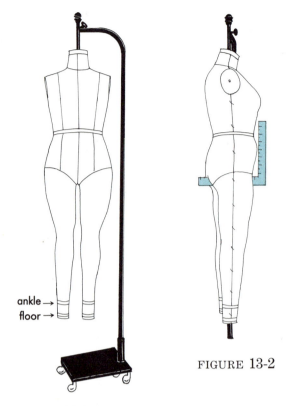

FIGURE 13-2

FIGURE 13-1

2. Cut muslin thread perfect.

3. Block and press muslin.

4. Identify grainlines.

   A. Measure in 6 inches from lengthwise edge to identify center front and center back lengthwise grain in pencil. (**Figure 13-3**)

   B. Crossmark waistline 2 inches below top edge at center front and center back. (**Figure 13-3**)

   C. At the center front measure down from the top edge 9 inches to identify the hip level. Pencil crosswise grain at hip level from center front to center back. (**Figure 13-3**)

   D. Measure down from waistline crossmark, length of crotch level. Pencil crosswise grain at crotch level from front to back lengthwise edges. (**Figure 13-3**)

   E. Fold muslin in half lengthwise. Crossmark and identify lengthwise grain down center of muslin. (**Figure 13-3**)

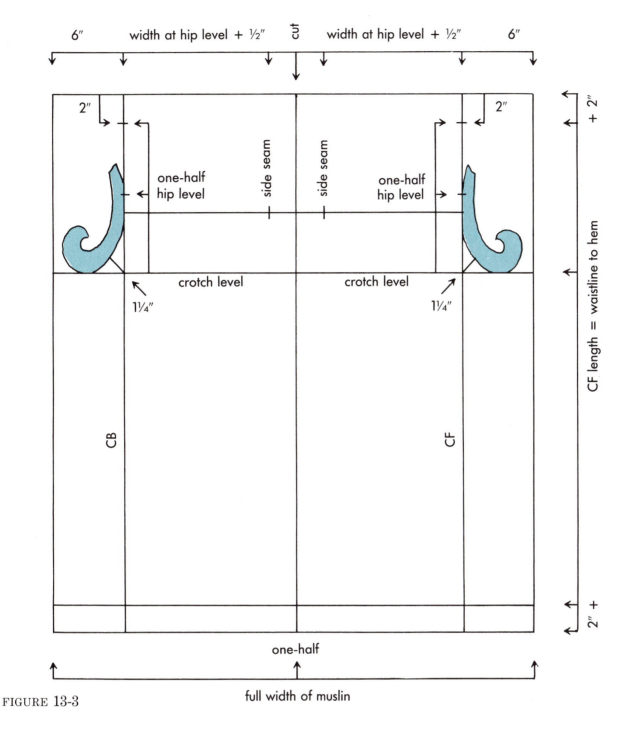

FIGURE 13-3

F. Crossmark one-half the crotch length at center front and back lengthwise grain. (**Figure 13-3**)

G. At the center front/back intersection at crotch level, measure up 1½ inches and identify a diagonal line at a 45° angle. (**Figure 13-3**)
Note The 45° diagonal line can measure 1¼ to 1½ inches.

H. Place the french curve with the outside edge along the center front touching the halfway crotch level crossmark, the 1½-inch diagonal line and crotch level. True the crotch curve. (**Figure 13-3**)

Repeat on back.

I. Add 1 inch seam allowance at crotch curve to top edge of muslin. Cut excess muslin.

J. Cut muslin in half to separate front and back. (**Figure 13-3**)

131

Draping the Front Pant

1. Pin center front lengthwise grain to center front of pants form at waistline, halfway crossmark and hip level. (**Figure 13-4**)

2. Smooth crosswise grain straight across hip level, pin at princess line and side seam taking and pinning ¼-inch ease on double between princess pin and side seam. (**Figure 13-4**) Be sure the crosswise grain at hip level is parallel to the floor and the ease is directed as a fold diagonally toward center front (see **Draping the Front Skirt, #3, page 88.**)

3. Keeping center front lengthwise grain straight (at right angles to the floor) and crotch curve through legs smooth, slash seam allowance as needed. Pin crotch level to inseam of pants form. (**Figure 13-5**)

4. At side seam, smooth muslin up from hip level and pin at waistline. (**Figure 13-4**)

5. Drape excess fullness across waistline as in **Draping the Front Skirt, #4–#12, pages 88–89** or distribute and pin excess fullness across waistline as gathers or style lines (dart tucks or tucks in combination with gathers). (**Figures 13-4, 13-6**)

Note When molding excess fullness at waistline, center front seam may shift off lengthwise grain.

6. Mark: (**Figures 13-6, 13-7**)

   A. Waistline and design details, crossmark intersection at center front.

   B. Side seam from hip level to waistline, crossmark intersections at waistline, crotch, knee and floor levels.

   C. Center front from halfway crossmark to waistline when not on lengthwise grain.

   D. Crossmark crotch level at inseam of pants form.

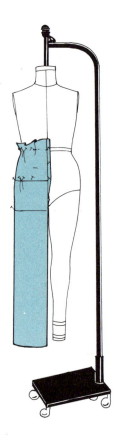

FIGURE 13-4

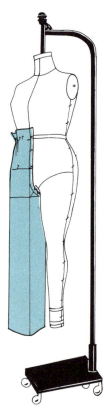

FIGURE 13-5

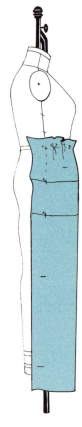

FIGURE 13-6

Trueing the Front Pant

1. Remove the front muslin from the pants form. (**Figure 13-7**)

2. True waistline darts and/or other stylized detail. (**Figure 13-8**)

3. True center front from halfway crossmark to waistline when not on lengthwise grain. (**Figure 13-8**)

4. True side seam blending marks from hip level to waistline with hip curve. (**Figure 13-8**)

5. Mark lengthwise grain at side seam from crossmark at hip level to bottom edge of muslin and from inseam crossmark at crotch level to bottom edge of muslin. (**Figure 13-8**)

6. Add 1 inch seam allowance at side seam and pants inseam. Cut excess muslin. (**Figure 13-8**)

7. Pin stylized detail at waistline closed.

8. Return front muslin to pants form. Be sure all marks are accurately pinned to pants form. At side seam sink pins completely into pants form at waistline, hip and crotch levels to keep seam allowance flat and molded to form. (**Figure 13-9**).

9. At crotch level pin inseam seam allowance to pants form to keep flat. (**Figure 13-9**)

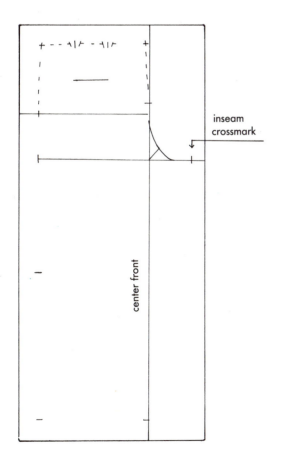

inseam crossmark

center front

FIGURE 13-7

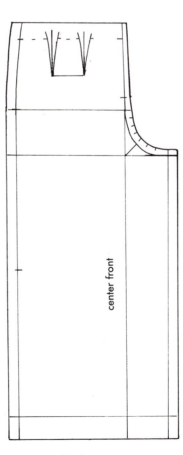

center front

FIGURE 13-8

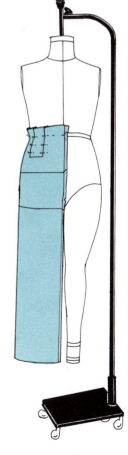

FIGURE 13-9

Draping the Back Pant

1. Pin center back lengthwise grain to center back of pants form at waistline, halfway crossmark and hip level, aligning crosswise grain at hip and crotch level with hip and crotch level of front muslin at side seam. (**Figure 13-10**)

2. At hip level, keep crosswise grain parallel to the floor from side seam to center back. Be sure to include and pin ease ¼ inch on double, between the princess line and side seam. (**Figure 13-10**)

3. Keeping the center back lengthwise grain straight and smooth from halfway pin to bottom edge, drape crotch curve through legs, aligning crotch level back over front at the inseam. Slash crotch curve seam allowance as needed. Crossmark and pin crotch inseam intersection. (**Figure 13-10**)

4. At side seam smooth muslin up from hip level, pin at waistline. (**Figure 13-10**)

5. At center back smooth muslin up from hip level to waistline; center back seam may shift off lengthwise grain. (**Figure 13-12**)

6. Distribute and pin excess fullness across waistline or style fullness in combination with a dart at princess line. (**Figure 13-10**)

7. **Mark: (Figures 13-11, 13-12)**

   A. Waistline and design details, crossmark intersection at center back.

   B. Directly from front muslin, mark side seam from hip level to waistline, crossmark intersections at waistline, crotch, knee and floor levels.

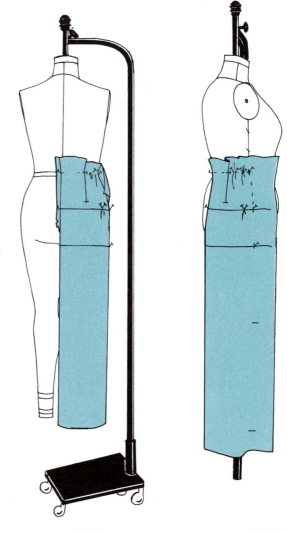

FIGURE 13-10   FIGURE 13-11

   C. Center back from halfway crossmark to waistline when not on lengthwise grain.

   D. Crossmark inseam directly from front muslin at crotch level.

134

Trueing the Back Pant

1. Remove the back muslin from the pants form. (**Figure 13-12**)

2. True waistline darts and/or other stylized details. (**Figure 13-13**)

3. True center back from halfway crossmark to waistline when not on lengthwise grain. (**Figure 13-13**)

4. True side seam blending marks from hip level to waistline with hip curve. (**Figure 13-13**)

5. Mark lengthwise grain at side seam from crossmark at hip level to bottom edge of muslin and from inseam crossmark at crotch level to bottom edge of muslin. (**Figure 13-13**)

   Note Pants may be tapered or shaped from this point (broken line in **Figures 13-14, 13-15**).

6. Add 1 inch seam allowance at side seam and pant inseam. Cut excess muslin. (**Figure 13-13**)

7. Remove front muslin from pants form.

8. Pin front and back pants muslin together at side seams, back over front matching waist-

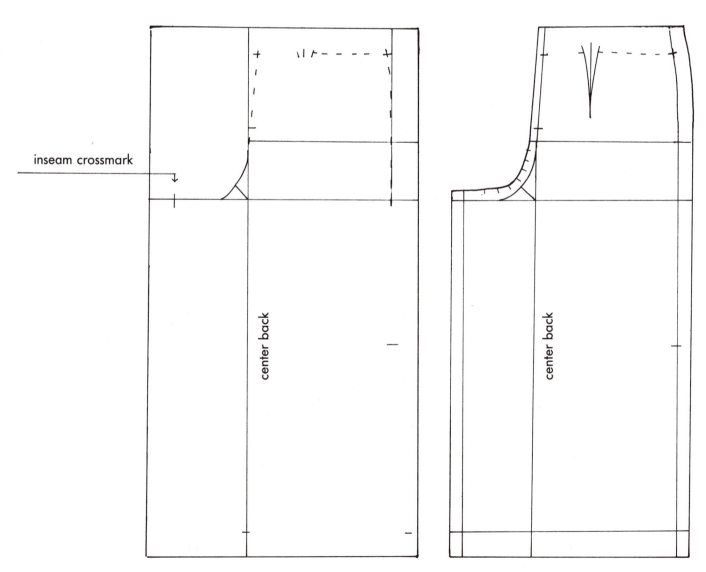

FIGURE 13-12   FIGURE 13-13

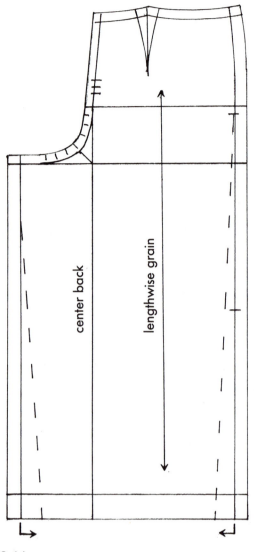

FIGURE 13-14

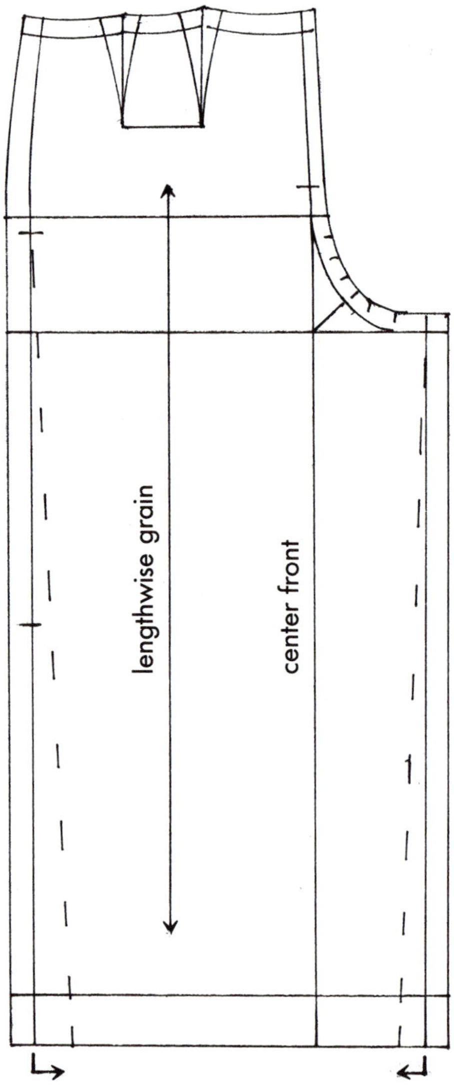

FIGURE 13-15

line, hip and crotch levels and knee and floor level crossmarks.

9. Pencil crosswise grain at floor level crossmarks from side seam to center front and back inseams.

10. Add 2 inches seam allowance. Cut excess muslin. (**Figures 13-14, 13-15**)

11. True waistline using hip curve (as in **Trueing the Back Skirt, #6, page 93**).

12. Pin pant inseams together back over front matching crotch and floor levels.

13. Return muslin to pants form for final checking. (**Figures 13-16, 13-17**)

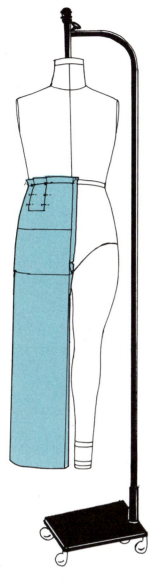

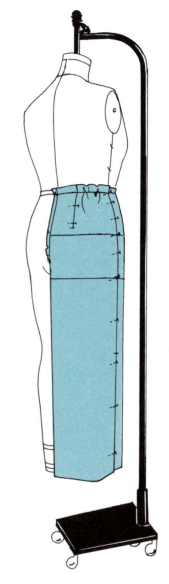

FIGURE 13-16

FIGURE 13-17

Preparing Muslin

1. Press carefully along grainline. True muslin.

2. On front bodice muslin, draw a line on the crosswise grainline from center front through the armhole/underarm intersection and from the waistline to the side seam. Repeat on back bodice muslin.

   Note Pull thread to obtain grainline if necessary.

Front & Back Slopers

Figure 14-1

1. Cut paper approximately 36″ × 28″.

2. Measure widest part of front and back muslin bodices (armhole/underarm intersections to center front and center back).

3. Use these measurements plus 4 inches and draw two parallel vertical lines. Identify *center front* and *center back* as illustrated.
   Note Check that lines are the same width at the top and bottom.

4. Draw a horizontal line at right angles to vertical lines through center of paper.

5. Measure distance between bust and waist levels at center front of front and back muslin bodices.

6. Use this measurement and on paper crossmark at center front and center back. Draw a line connecting crossmarks to identify waist level.
   Note Waist level must be parallel to bust level and at right angles to center front and back.

Figure 14-2

1. Place front bodice muslin on paper matching lengthwise grainlines center front and crosswise grainlines at bust and waist levels. Pin. Smooth remainder of muslin into position. Pin. Repeat on back bodice muslin.

   Note Be careful not to stretch muslin at grainlines or at cut edges. When muslin patterns are secured, check that all grainlines are at right angles to each other. See illustration for direction of grainline at armholes and underarms.

2. With tracing wheel, trace finished seamlines, darts and crossmarks onto paper.

3. Remove muslin. Pencil all traced lines. True darts and seams. Cut excess paper from seamlines.

   Note Pencil lines should be removed by cutting. Cut next to line inside of sloper.

crosswise grain = 36″

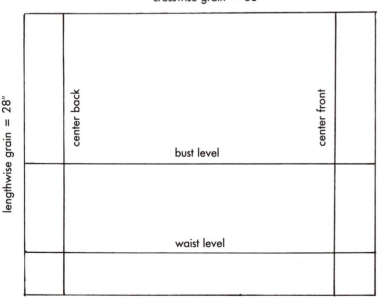

FIGURE 14-1

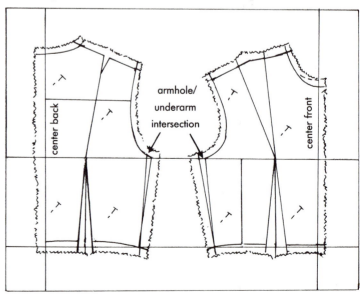

FIGURE 14-2

Skirt & Torso Slopers

The principles for transferring and trueing muslin patterns onto paper for skirt and torso slopers (**Figures 14-3, 14-4**) are the same as for front and back bodice slopers.

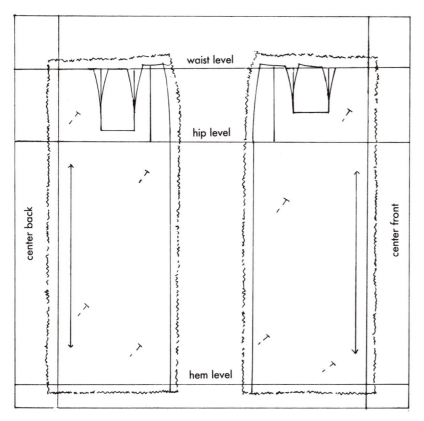

FIGURE 14-3

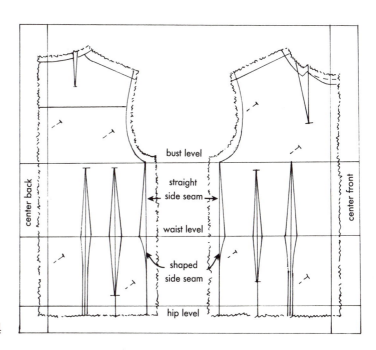

FIGURE 14-4

139

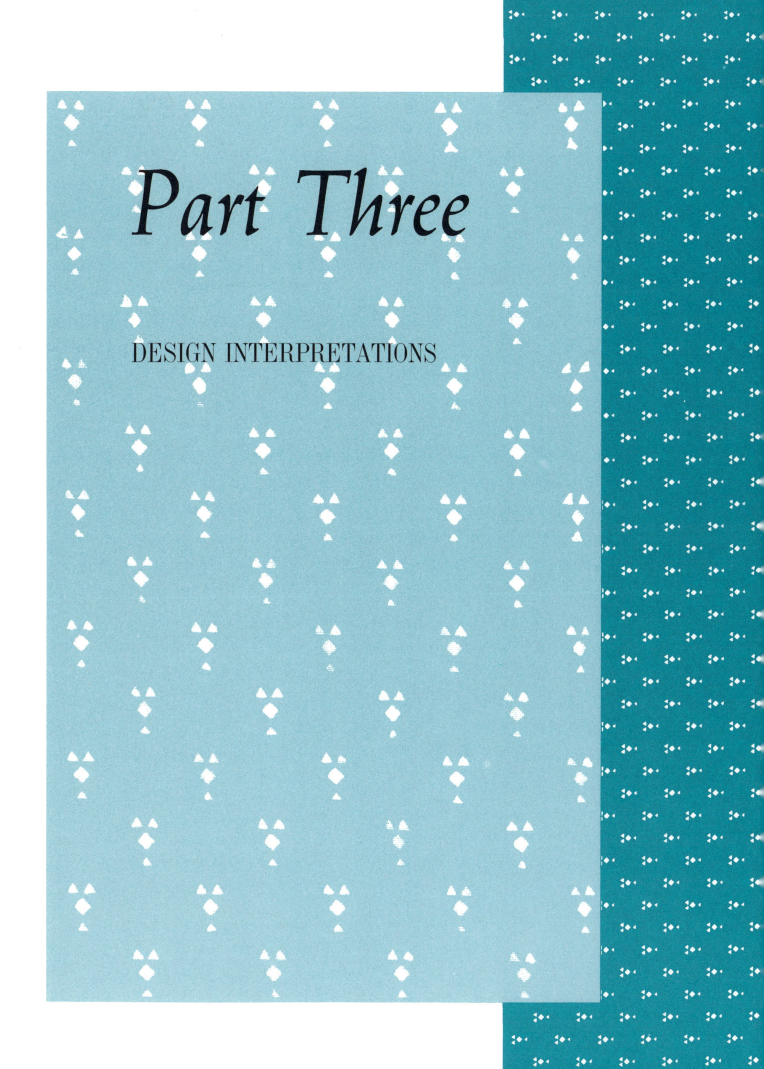

Part Three

DESIGN INTERPRETATIONS

Design Interpretations

Developing and understanding the principles of design as they relate to the ample figure, and mastering the principles and techniques of draping and flat patternmaking will permit you to design more unusual and complicated patterns. It is necessary to practice developing patterns for designs of varying degrees of difficulty, to gain confidence and to design any pattern desired.

The dress form itself can be a challenge to inventiveness. It provides a three-dimensional shape on which to experiment with space divisions and fabric. The dress form suggests where it will be advantageous to extend or confine the silhouette of the design, and shows the merits of curved or straight lines, and of horizontal or vertical dominance in line direction. Inconsistency in the scale of major space divisions, or inappropriateness of detail to the entire figure becomes apparent at once. The challenge is to retain the ample figure's most pleasing attributes, to emphasize them through the lines of the garment and to modify the less desirable proportions by subtle illusion, maintaining good taste.

On the following pages, designs are interpreted utilizing the muslin sloper most adaptable to the silhouette. Style tape is used to outline the style lines and details on the dress form. Design lines and details are transferred to the flat paper sloper maintaining the proportion as it relates to the three-dimensional figure. Flat patternmaking methods facilitate the completion of a pattern.

The quality of design and fit is improved when flat patterns are developed from style lines that have been proportioned on the dress form and marked on the draped sloper. It combines fit and accuracy of proportion of the draped sloper with the speed and exactness of flat patternmaking.

Patterns, whether developed through draping or flat patternmaking, must be trued and tested in muslin for style, harmony of line, fit and proportion on the dress form or live model before cutting the sample pattern in fabric. If the pattern is cut in fabric, ample seam allowances must be added to allow for fitting or style-line changes desired.

Volume production patterns are tested in both muslin and dress fabric. Patterns are first cut in muslin, fitted and corrected before original paper patterns are created. Patterns are then cut in dress fabric and assembled following mass production procedures. The first garment is called a duplicate.

Converting the Bodice Sloper to the Straight Side Seam Torso Sloper

To develop this design convert the basic bodice sloper to straight side seam torso sloper.

1. Estimate yardage.

   Lengthwise Grain Measure center front and back of bodice slopers plus 12 inches.

   Crosswise Grain Measure widest part of front and back bodice slopers plus 6 inches.

2. Use this measurement and cut muslin thread perfect on the lengthwise and crosswise grains.

3. Block muslin until grain perfect and press.

4. Identify grainlines.

   A. Measure in 1 inch from both sides of the cut lengthwise edge and identify the center front and center back lengthwise grains.

   B. Measure down 5 inches from the top edge of center front lengthwise grain and crossmark center front/neckline intersection. On muslin place paper front bodice down matching center front/neckline intersections, crossmark bust and waist levels at center front. Remove paper pattern. Identify crosswise grain at bust and waist levels from center front to center back in pencil.

5. Place paper front bodice on muslin matching center front lengthwise and crosswise grains at bust and waist levels. Pin in position to secure.

6. Mark at 1-inch intervals all seamlines and intersections.

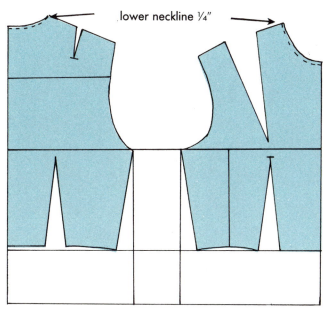

lower neckline ¼"

FIGURE 15-1

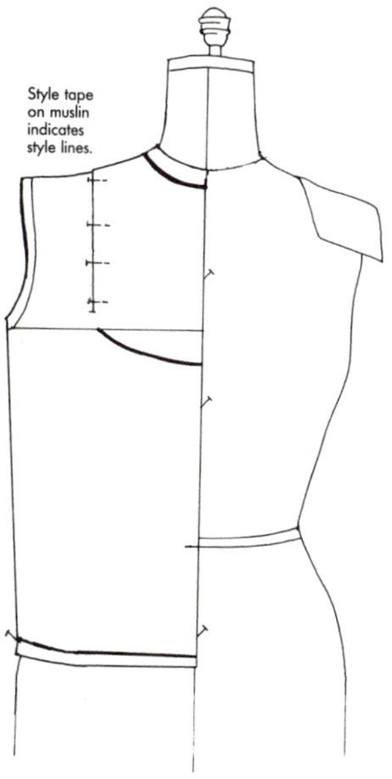

Style tape on muslin indicates style lines.

cut 2

FIGURE 15-2 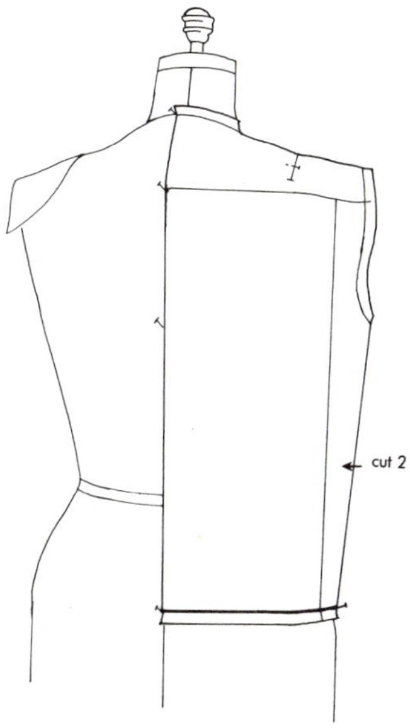   FIGURE 15-3

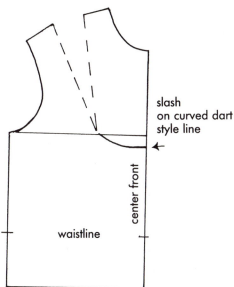

slash
on curved dart
style line

center front

waistline

FIGURE 15-4

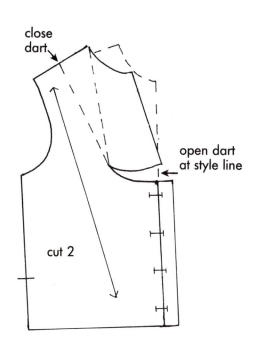

close
dart

open dart
at style line

cut 2

FIGURE 15-5

7. With tracing wheel and carbon paper, trace shoulder dart. Remove paper bodice pattern. True all seamlines and shoulder dart in pencil.

8. To identify straight side seam, mark lengthwise grain bust level at armhole intersection to bottom of muslin.

9. Repeat for back torso muslin.

10. Add seam allowances to front and back torso patterns. Cut excess muslin.

11. Pin front and back muslin patterns together. Return muslin torso to dress form for final checking.

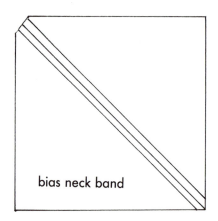

FIGURE 15-8

To develop skirt use
the basic skirt sloper.

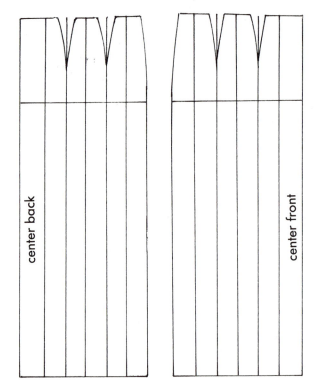

center back

center front

FIGURE 15-9

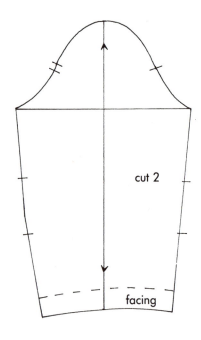

cut 2

facing

FIGURE 15-6

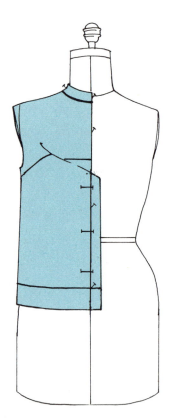

FIGURE 15-7

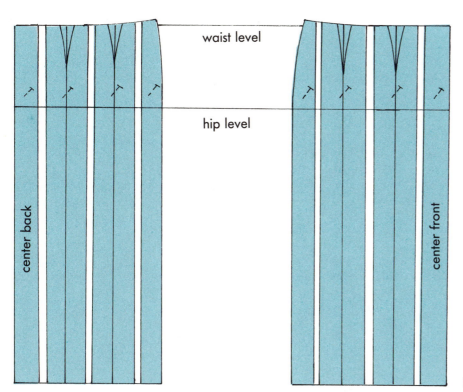

waist level

hip level

center back

center front

FIGURE 15-10

FIGURE 15-14

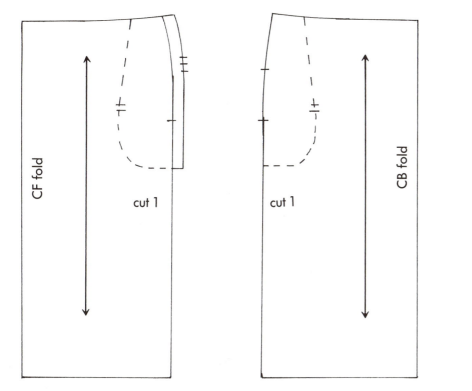

CF fold

cut 1

cut 1

CB fold

FIGURE 15-11

FIGURE 15-12

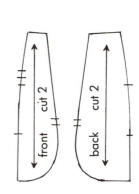

front

cut 2

cut 2

back

FIGURE 15-13

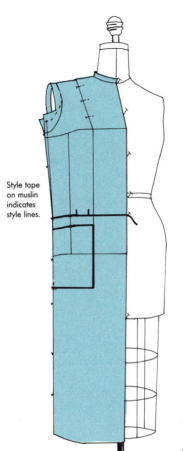

Style tape
on muslin
indicates
style lines.

FIGURE 16-1

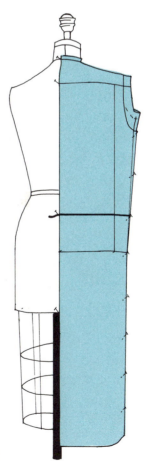

To develop this design use muslin shift sloper.   FIGURE 16-2

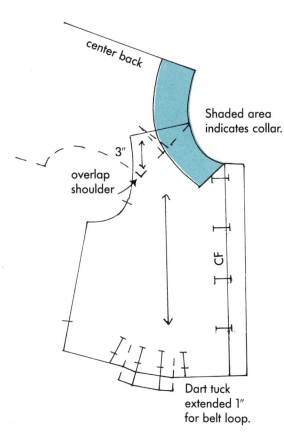

center back

3″

overlap shoulder

Shaded area indicates collar.

CF

Dart tuck extended 1″ for belt loop.

FIGURE 16-5

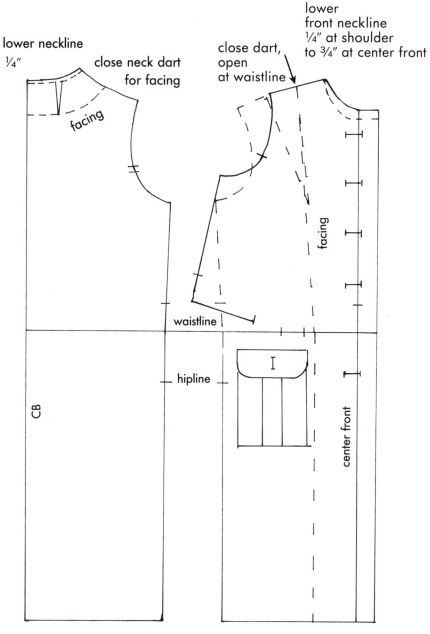

lower neckline ¼″

close neck dart for facing

facing

close dart, open at waistline

lower front neckline ¼″ at shoulder to ¾″ at center front

facing

waistline

hipline

CB

center front

FIGURE 16-3

FIGURE 16-4

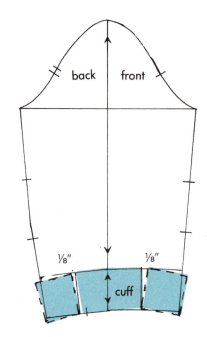

back

front

⅛″

⅛″

cuff

FIGURE 16-6

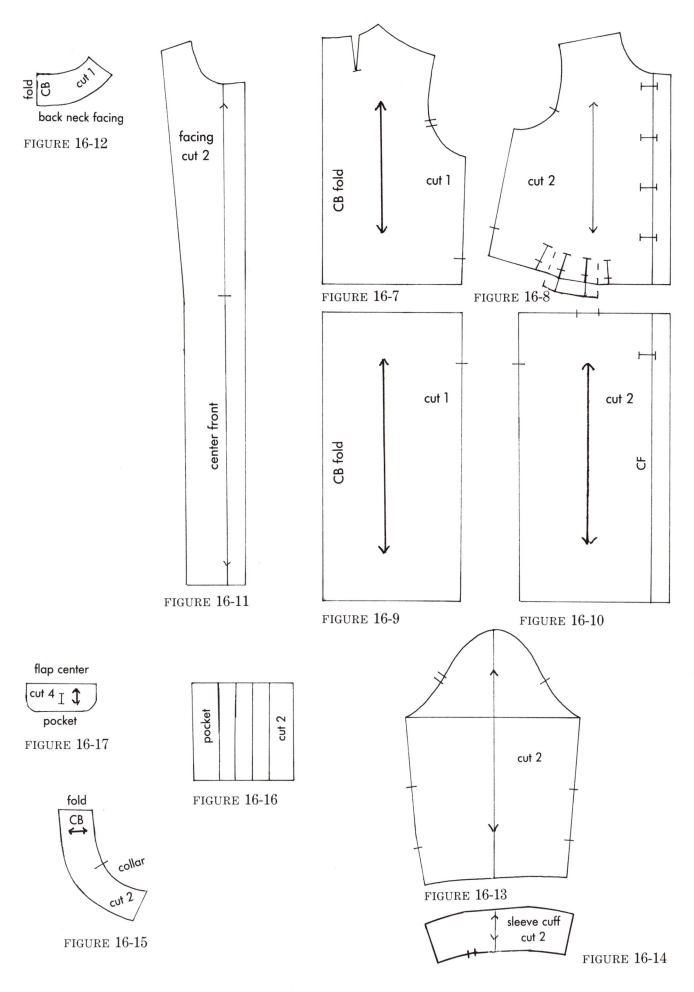

fold CB cut 1
back neck facing

FIGURE 16-12

facing cut 2

center front

FIGURE 16-11

CB fold cut 1

FIGURE 16-7

cut 2

FIGURE 16-8

CB fold cut 1

FIGURE 16-9

cut 2 CF

FIGURE 16-10

flap center
cut 4 I
pocket

FIGURE 16-17

pocket cut 2

FIGURE 16-16

fold CB collar cut 2

FIGURE 16-15

cut 2

FIGURE 16-13

sleeve cuff cut 2

FIGURE 16-14

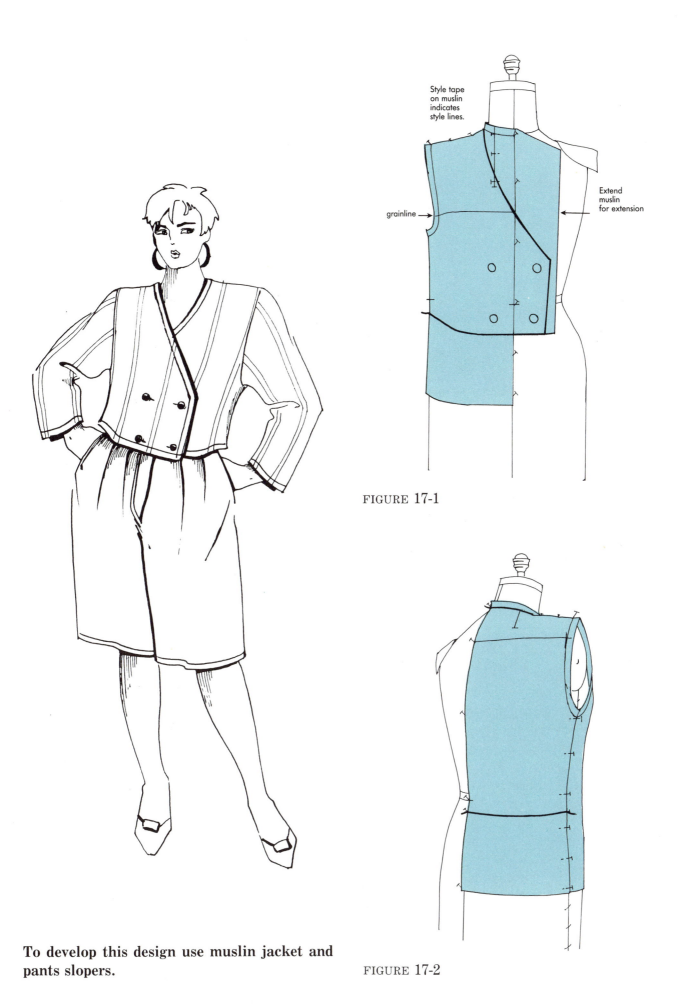

Style tape on muslin indicates style lines.

grainline →

← Extend muslin for extension

FIGURE 17-1

To develop this design use muslin jacket and pants slopers.

FIGURE 17-2

153

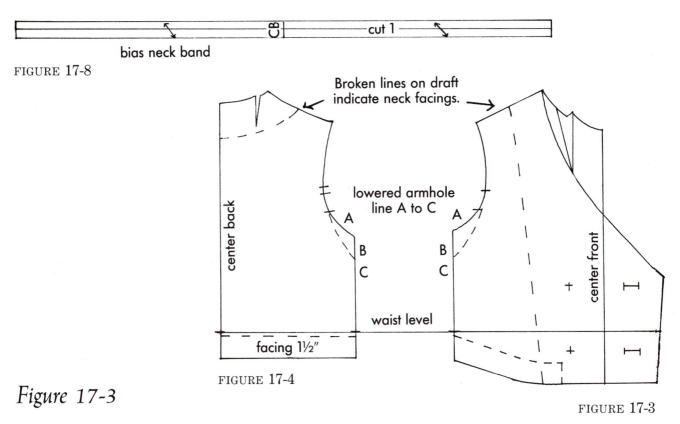

bias neck band

FIGURE 17-8

FIGURE 17-4

Broken lines on draft indicate neck facings.

Figure 17-3

FIGURE 17-3

1. Measure down depth of jacket lowered arm-hole B to C.

2. Mark with dotted line jacket lowered arm-hole A to C.

3. Measure distance A to B from biceps/under-arm intersection along capline, mark D.

4. Square a right angle line from biceps level up to capline point D.

5. At front and back biceps/underarm seam in-tersections, measure up and out the distance of jacket lowered armhole, B to C. Draw a parallel line.

6. Cut sleeve on biceps level to right angle line and up to D.

7. Pivot wedge shape up to raised biceps line.

8. From point D measure out on raised biceps line the distance of jacket lowered armhole line (A to C).

9. Blend a new curved underarm seamline end-ing above elbow level.

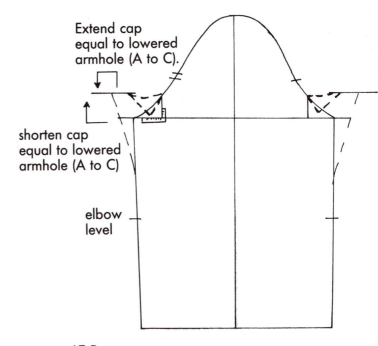

FIGURE 17-5

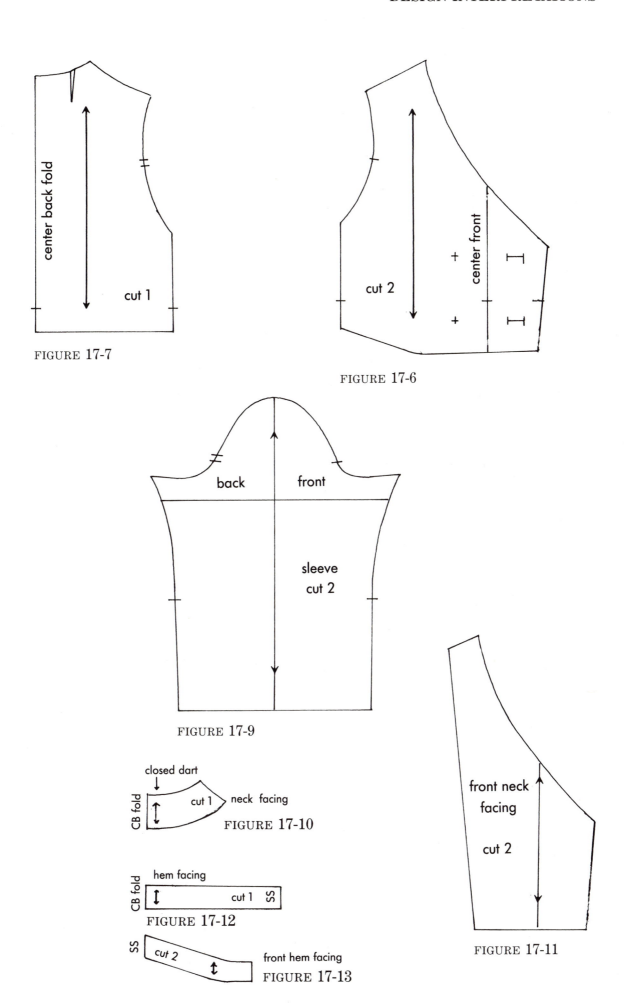

center back fold

cut 1

FIGURE 17-7

cut 2

center front

FIGURE 17-6

back   front

sleeve
cut 2

FIGURE 17-9

closed dart

CB fold

cut 1   neck facing

FIGURE 17-10

front neck
facing

cut 2

FIGURE 17-11

hem facing

CB fold

cut 1   SS

FIGURE 17-12

SS   cut 2

front hem facing

FIGURE 17-13

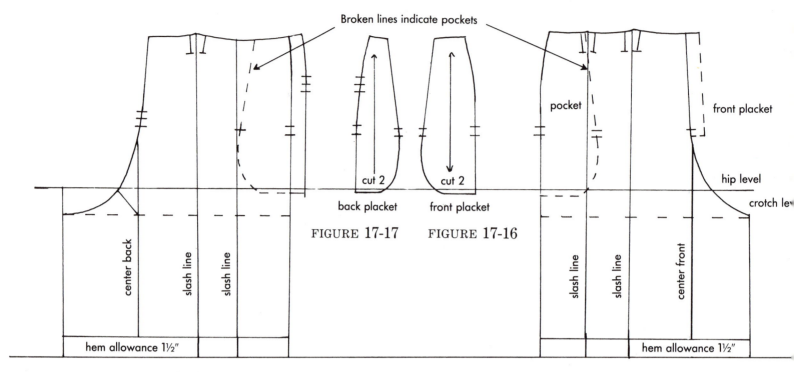

Broken lines indicate pockets

cut 2

back placket

FIGURE 17-17

cut 2

front placket

FIGURE 17-16

pocket

front placket

hip level

crotch le

center back

slash line

slash line

slash line

slash line

center front

hem allowance 1½"

hem allowance 1½"

FIGURE 17-15

FIGURE 17-14

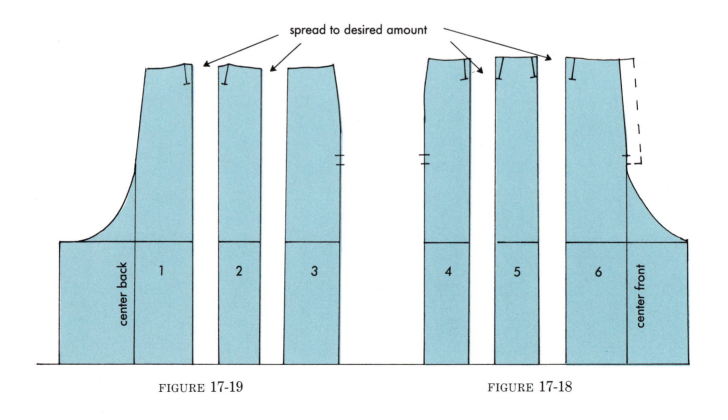

spread to desired amount

center back

1

2

3

4

5

6

center front

FIGURE 17-19

FIGURE 17-18

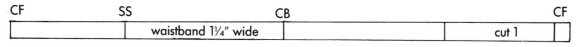

CF   SS   CB   CF

| waistband 1¼" wide | | cut 1 | |

FIGURE 17-22

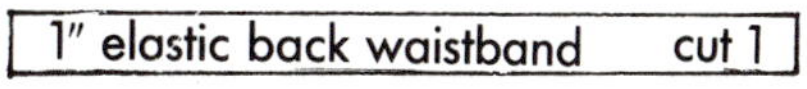

| 1" elastic back waistband   cut 1 | FIGURE 17-23

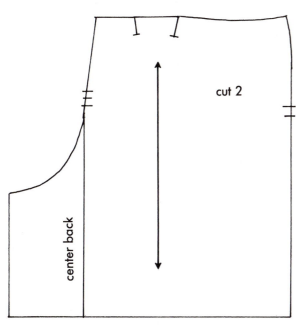

cut 2

center back

FIGURE 17-21

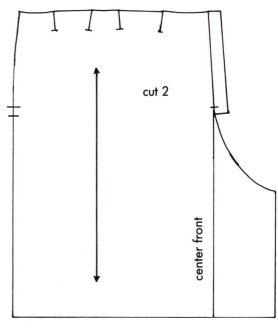

cut 2

center front

FIGURE 17-20

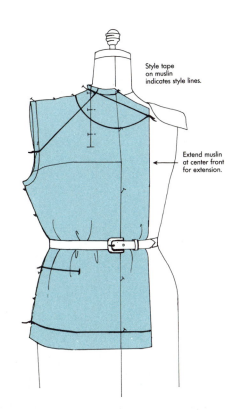

Style tape on muslin indicates style lines.

Extend muslin at center front for extension.

FIGURE 18-1

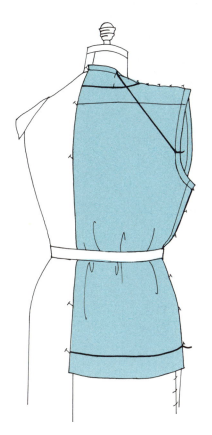

To develop this design use muslin straight jacket and skirt slopers.

FIGURE 18-2

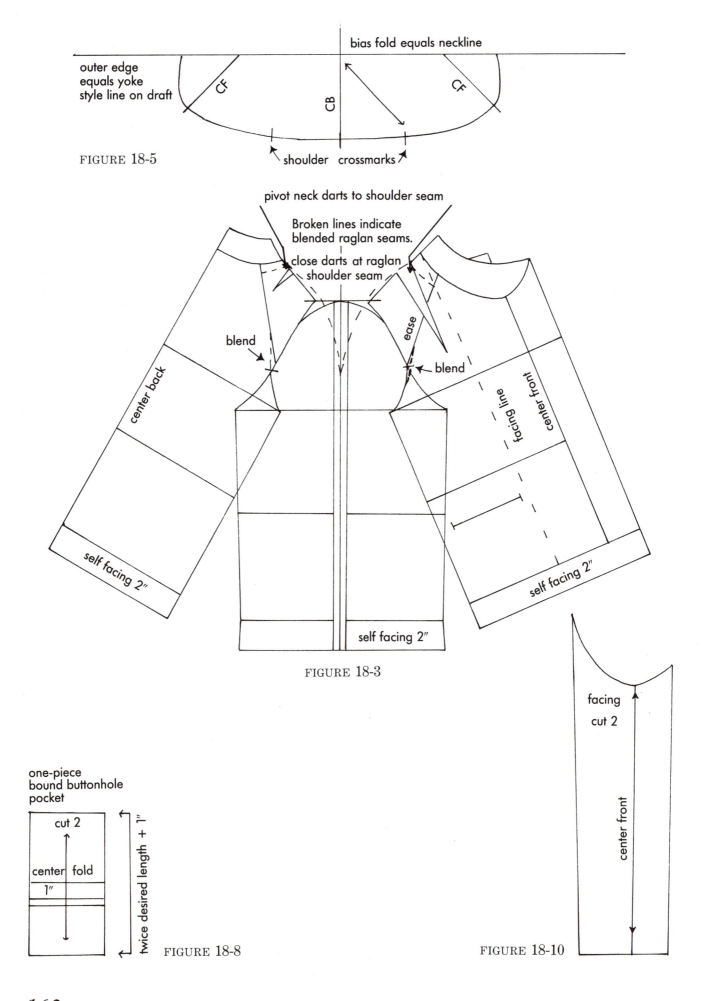

outer edge
equals yoke
style line on draft

bias fold equals neckline

CF

CB

CF

shoulder crossmarks

FIGURE 18-5

pivot neck darts to shoulder seam

Broken lines indicate
blended raglan seams.

close darts at raglan
shoulder seam

center back

blend

ease

blend

facing line

center front

self facing 2"

self facing 2"

self facing 2"

FIGURE 18-3

facing

cut 2

center front

FIGURE 18-10

one-piece
bound buttonhole
pocket

cut 2

center fold

1"

twice desired length + 1"

FIGURE 18-8

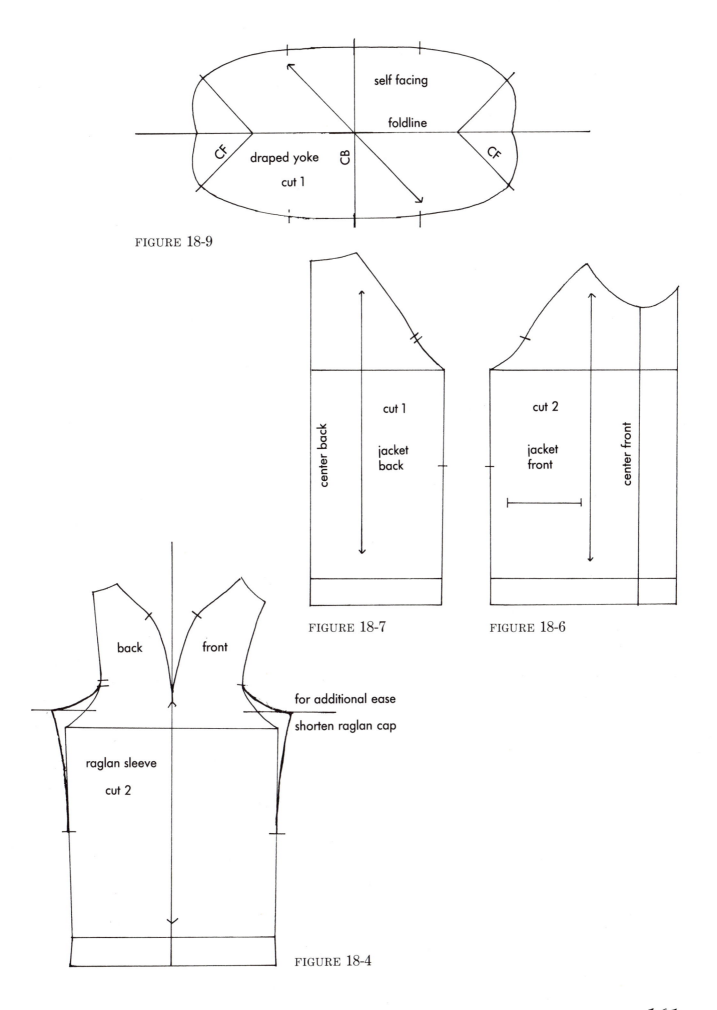

FIGURE 18-9

self facing

foldline

CF

draped yoke

cut 1

CB

CF

FIGURE 18-7

center back

cut 1

jacket back

FIGURE 18-6

cut 2

jacket front

center front

back

front

for additional ease

shorten raglan cap

raglan sleeve

cut 2

FIGURE 18-4

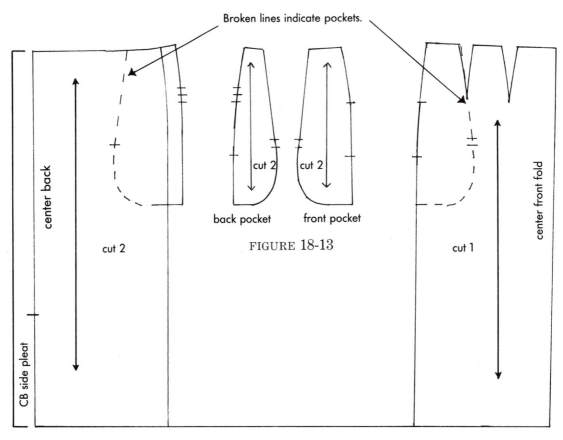

Broken lines indicate pockets.

center back

CB side pleat

cut 2

FIGURE 18-12

back pocket   front pocket

cut 2   cut 2

FIGURE 18-13

cut 1

center front fold

FIGURE 18-11

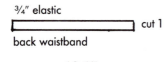

¾" elastic

cut 1

back waistband

FIGURE 18-15

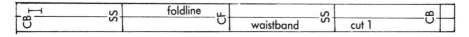

CB   SS   foldline   CF   SS   CB

waistband   cut 1

FIGURE 18-14

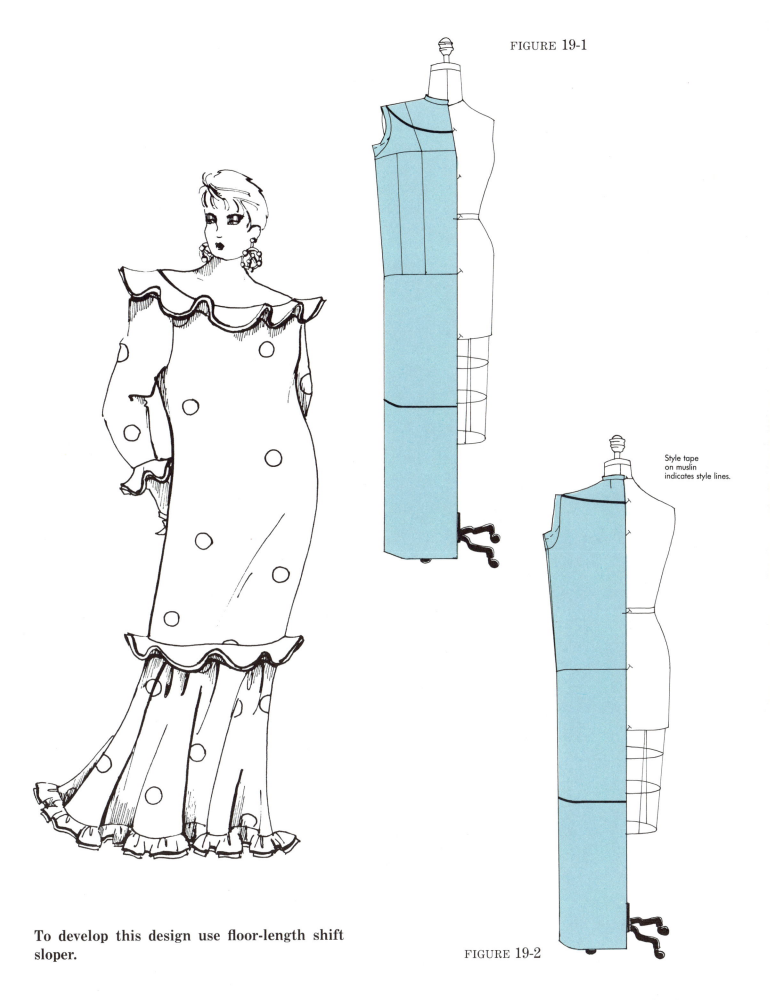

FIGURE 19-1

Style tape
on muslin
indicates style lines.

FIGURE 19-2

To develop this design use floor-length shift sloper.

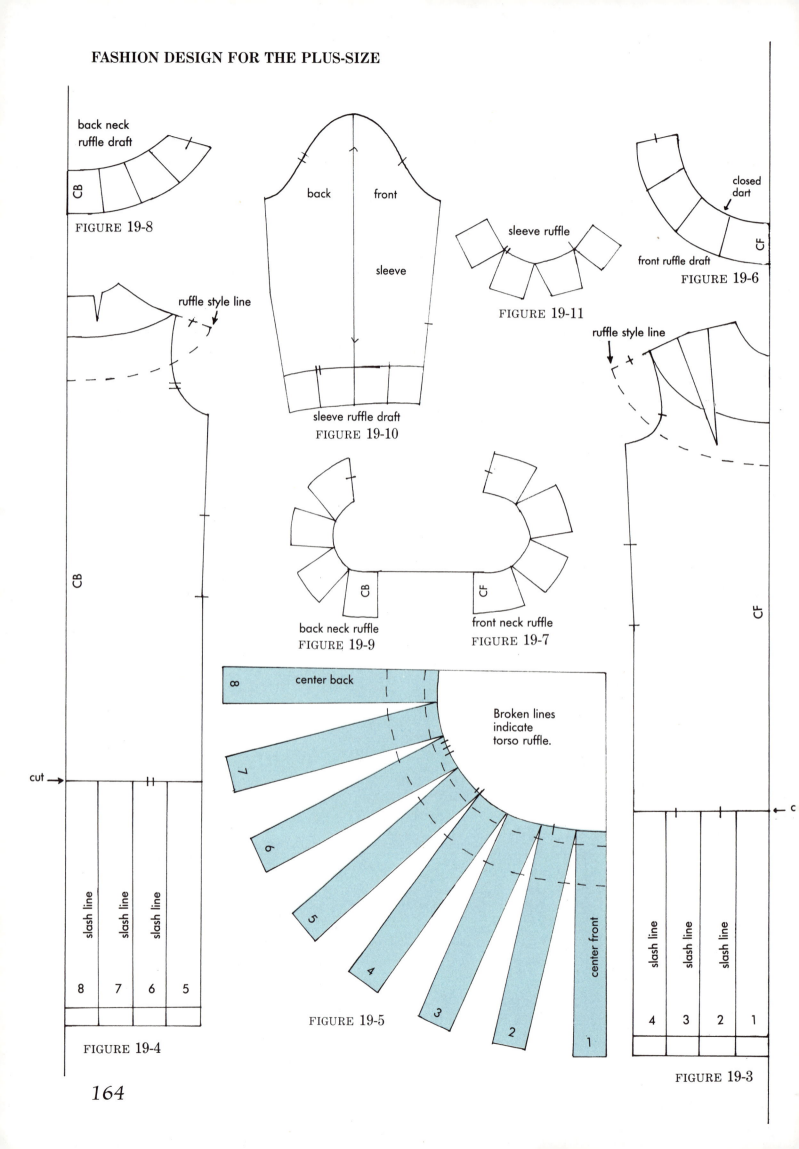

back neck
ruffle draft

CB

FIGURE 19-8

ruffle style line

CB

cut →

slash line

slash line

slash line

| 8 | 7 | 6 | 5 |

FIGURE 19-4

back

front

sleeve

sleeve ruffle draft

FIGURE 19-10

sleeve ruffle

FIGURE 19-11

closed
dart

front ruffle draft

CF

FIGURE 19-6

ruffle style line

CF

slash line

slash line

slash line

| 4 | 3 | 2 | 1 |

FIGURE 19-3

CB

back neck ruffle

FIGURE 19-9

CF

front neck ruffle

FIGURE 19-7

8

center back

7

6

5

4

3

2

1

center front

Broken lines
indicate
torso ruffle.

FIGURE 19-5

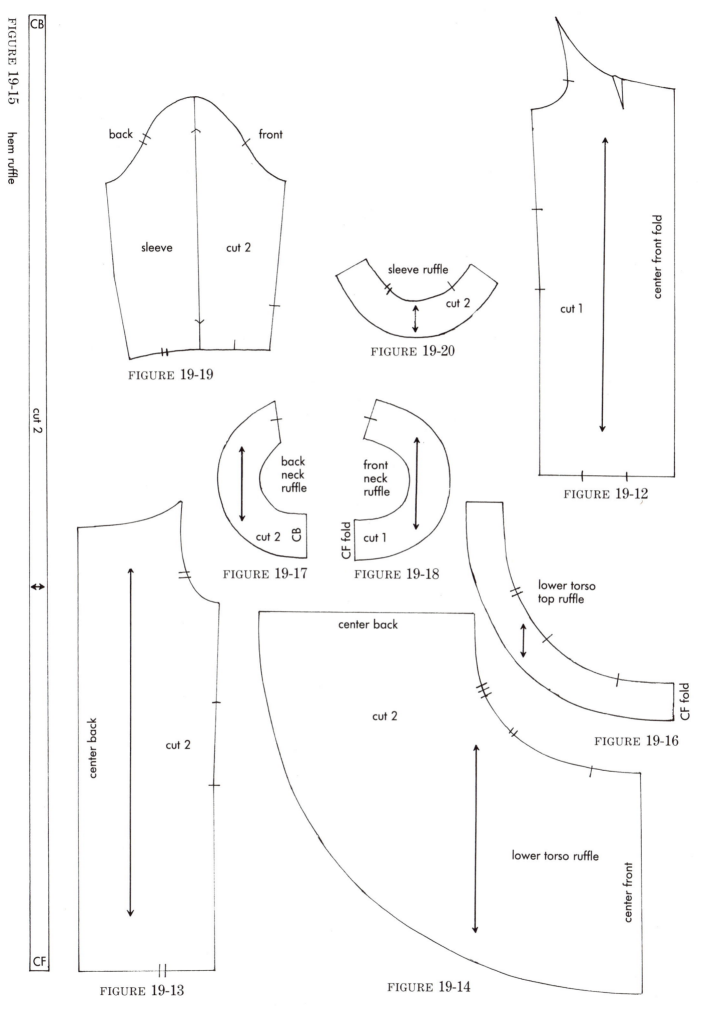

FIGURE 19-15   hem ruffle

CB

cut 2

CF

back   front

sleeve   cut 2

FIGURE 19-19

sleeve ruffle

cut 2

FIGURE 19-20

center front fold

cut 1

FIGURE 19-12

back neck ruffle

cut 2   CB

FIGURE 19-17

front neck ruffle

CF fold   cut 1

FIGURE 19-18

lower torso top ruffle

CF fold

FIGURE 19-16

center back

cut 2

center back

cut 2

FIGURE 19-13

lower torso ruffle

center front

FIGURE 19-14

165

Part Four

GRADING FOR THE
PLUS-SIZE FIGURE

GRADING BODICES, SKIRTS,
SLEEVES, PANTS

HOW THE PLUS-SIZE BODY
PROPORTIONS INCREASE PER SIZE

IDENTIFYING PLUS-SIZE
BODY CHECKPOINTS

PUBLISHED SOURCES
OF FASHION TRENDS

Grading for the Plus-Size Figure

Grading* as practiced in the garment industry, is the art of increasing or decreasing uniformly the size of the master pattern without changing the style of the garment. It is the ability of changing a size 18W, for example, to a well-fitting size 20W, without sacrificing the style or proportions of the garment. Accurate grading is especially significant to the plus-size customer as it improves her chances of finding a garment of her choice in a size and style pleasing to her particular figure.

The body measurements of given sizes vary from one manufacturer to another, a confusing problem to the plus-size customer. Although the American Society for Testing and Materials is working at the request of the Federal Government to establish new size standards for American women's clothing, it is meeting resistance from manufacturers who have all but ignored

standards for years, preferring to establish clothes and sizes in their own image. Standards were developed in 1940 and were strictly followed for many years. These measurements are obsolete because the shape of the American woman has changed noticeably over the last 45 years. Manufacturers resist standards for other reasons as well. Many add inches to each size category because they want women to think they are wearing a size smaller on the theory that women are more likely to buy a garment if they think it is a size smaller than they normally wear. In addition, manufacturers contend too, that size is one thing that sets them apart in the marketplace that it allows them to differentiate their product. Right now a size can mean whatever a manufacturer wants it to mean. There is no consensus on a fixed set of standard measurements that can be used as a general basis, making for a great deal of variation in the measurements currently used. Measurements are influenced and modified by manufacturers of designer clothing, of dress forms and by consumer complaints and suggestions. The American Society for Testing

---

* A complete study of grading, however, is much too extensive a study for coverage in this text. For further information see, *Grading Techniques for Modern Design*, Jeanne Price and Bernard Zamkoff; *Pattern Grading*, M. Rohr.

Stores, firms OK standardizing larger sizes to two categories

NEW YORK — Manufacturers and retailers attending the National Retail Merchants Association's symposium on sizing for large-size women's apparel Wednesday voted unanimously to approve a standardization of terminology.

Under the new system, some 16 different size ranges will be reduced to two, based on numbers currently used in misses' sizing. The first size range would go from size 14W to 32W — "W" designating women's — and the second range would run from 14WP and 32WP, standing for the women's petite."

For the large-size equivalent of women's small, medium, large and extra-large, 1X, 2X, 3X and 4X will be used.

The old system includes half sizes, for short, heavier women, generally perceived as an older woman category, and large sizes. However, within the large-size parameters have been three ranges of dress sizes, blouses that do not correspond to bust sizes, bottoms that do not designate waist size and no way of comparing sizes from one apparel item to another. Confusion has permeated the market, according to all 17 panelists speaking at the conference.

The session — attended by more than 200 retailers from department stores, small and larger chain specialty stores, buying office executives and manufacturers — was held Wednesday morning at the Barbizon Plaza Hotel here.

Originally scheduled to run from 9 a.m. to 1 p.m., the conference ended 45 minutes early because participants were eager to bring the proposal to a vote. Before the vote, panelists, representing a wide cross-section of the industry, put forth their arguments regarding the need for standardization.

Attendees at the conference included representatives of Sears, Roebuck & Co., Allied Stores Corp., J.C. Penney Co., Bloomingdale's, Lane Bryant, Carter Hawley Hale Stores, Inc., Montgomery Ward & Co., The May Department Stores Co., Federated Department Stores, Lord & Taylor and Mercantile Stores Co.

The next step will be for the committee to send all large-size resources an information packet describing the results of the meeting, a conversion chart and an explanation of how the proposal will be implemented. According to Ernestine Linn, president of the Carr Specialties division of Carr Buying, who chaired the conference, it will be up to the retailers to ask their manufacturers to comply with the system. She emphasized that this does not change the specifications of the apparel being made, only the nomenclature in distinguishing those sizes.

Apparel will probably be double-ticketed for the first few seasons to ease the transition, according to Linn, with the first items bearing the new nomenclature appearing in the stores for spring. Well-posted conversion chart, signing and in-store education of personnel and consumers are vital to the system's success, she emphasized.

— EILEEN BRILL

Reprinted by permission of Women's Wear Daily, August 15, 1985, Copyright 1985, Fairchild Publications.

Conference on large sizes agrees to standardization

By EILEEN B. BRILL

NEW YORK — The standardization of sizing in the large-size market will mean more dollars for the already booming category, according to many participants at the sizing conference held last week at the Barbizon Plaza Hotel here. The conference was sponsored by the National Retail Merchants Association.

Since many large-size women have been buying in the misses' category, the switchover to a nomenclature modeled after misses' size — instead of numbers that can run from 34 to 52 — will make shopping more understandable. According to Joseph Ferri, vice president of Special Image, a specialty store based in Closter, N.J. and a panelist at the conference, seven out of 10 large-size women were not always in that category.

Attendees at the meeting voted unanimously to standardize sizing terminology. The new system would reduce size ranges from 16 to two, based on numbers used in misses' sizing. (For details, see page 18, Aug. 15).

Richard Bernstein, president of Harve Benard Woman, predicted his sales will increase 25 percent after the sizing changeover.

"The suit and coat business is grossly underdeveloped, although the need for career-oriented apparel for large-size working women is increasing," he noted. "We need to make it easier for these women to respond to our product."

Mary Duffy, president of Big Beauties, Inc., modeling agency, pointed out that psychologically, women will actually be more flattered shopping large-sizes than misses'. With the conversion specifications, a woman buying a 16 misses' size will be a 14W under the new system.

But even with the sizing terminology issue apparently settled at the conference, new problems in the industry surfaced. While panelists clearly indicated that the change referred to standardizing terminology only, several attendees stated the need for standardization of body type specifications as well. In other words, which women can wear a size 22W skirt varies enormously depending on which company is producing the item.

However, others argued that cutting the apparel in a certain way is part of the craft of the manufacturer and the reason why customers buy from one company rather than another.

Panelists also addressed the psychological aspects of the size 12 woman who gains several pounds and becomes a size 34. Many of these women, while actually large-size shoppers, will continue to squeeze into misses' apparel to avoid the huge jump in size. Several panelists pointed out that while some stores carry misses' sizes as large as 16 or 18, the selection is significantly less than in their smaller sizes. Once women are persuaded to shop in the large-size stores or departments, the wider variety of apparel may tempt them to make more purchases.

To impose specifications, is "tremendously presumptuous of any group," according to Sy Finkelstein, president of Sy's Unlimited of Southfield, Mich.

This and other issues will be discussed further at the next NRMA's large-size conference, to be held this November at the Barbizon Plaza Hotel.

Reprinted by permission of Women's Wear Daily, August 19, 1985, Copyright 1985, Fairchild Publications.

---

and Materials is presently collecting the measurements of thousands of American women. Their goal: to establish new size standards for American clothing. They are trying to be the voice of reason; the voice of sanity.

As of 1986, sizing for plus-size women's apparel will consist of size ranges based on numbers currently used in missy sizing. The first size range would go from 14W to 26W—"W" designating women's. The second range would run from 14WP to 26WP—"WP" standing for women's petite.

A thorough knowledge of how the body changes from one size to another and a complete understanding of the ample figure measurements are basic to the study of grading principles as they relate to the plus-size figure. The following pages provide definitions and information of grading terms commonly used, illustrations identifying the body, diagrams and guides to illustrate the body from one size to the next.

Grading begins with the sample size pattern often referred to as the *master pattern*. The accuracy of the master pattern is crucial for successful results in sizing patterns. The master pattern represents the manufacturer's initial or *first pattern* from which duplicates are made. It is essential to maintain the style lines, proportion and fit of the master pattern as it is graded up or down from one size to another. The substance of grading a pattern is not only to make the necessary increases in width and length of the pattern for each size, but to retain the original style features and proportions of the design for all sizes.

Basic Grading Terms

Grade

To increase or decrease a measurement between sizes. The grade varies according to type of measurement—circumference, length or width. To find the grade for women's sizes the measurement of the bust circumference of a size 14W and 16W is taken. The difference between the two sizes becomes the grade. For example: a women's size 14, bust measurement is 39½ inches; a size 16, bust measurement is 41 inches. The difference is 1½ inches, and becomes the grade between a size 14W and 16W. A size 18W, bust measurement is 43 inches. The difference, 2 inches from 16W, becomes the grade between a size 16W and 18W and in remaining sizes up to 26W.

Each front and back pattern is one-fourth of the circumference measurement. Therefore, a 2-inch grade increases or decreases the width of each front and back pattern ½-inch per size. A 1½-inch grade increases or decreases the width of each front and back pattern ⅜-inch per size.

Length Grade

The length grade denotes how much should be added to the length of the pattern per size. The difference between the length measurements per size become the grade per size for a length measurement.

Width Grade

The width grade denotes the measurement to be added to the cross body areas (shoulder, chest, bust, waist and hip levels) to increase the width of each front and back pattern.

Standard Grade

Standard grade measurements *do not* change from one size to the next. The standard grade measurements in a bodice are the shoulder slope, neck, armhole depth, side seam, apex, dart length and the length grade in a skirt.

Changeable Grades

Changeable grade measurements are not constant and *change* from one size to the next. The changeable grade measurements include the bust level and those areas dependent upon it, shoulder, waistline, hip, and biceps level of the sleeve. The changeable measurements are noted by an asterisk (*) on the **Guides to Grading.** The Guides consider the measurements of all the areas of the body that have changeable grades per size as well as those areas that grade a standard amount per size.

VOLUNTARY NOMENCLATURE FOR
WOMEN'S PLUS-SIZE APPAREL*

PROPOSED PLUS-SIZE PETITE RANGE	12WP	14WP	16WP	18WP	20WP	22WP	24WP	26WP	28WP	30WP	32WP
Existing Sizes & Conversions											
Tops	—	14½	16½	18½	20½	22½	24½	26½	28½	30½	32½
	—	14P	16P	18P	20P	22P	24P	26P	28P	30P	32P
	—	34P	36P	38P	40P	42P	44P	46P	48P	50P	52P
Bottoms	—	14½	16½	18½	20½	22½	24½	26½	28½	30½	32½
	—	28P	30P	32P	34P	36P	38P	40P	42P	44P	46P
Sweaters**	—	—	—	—	—	—	—	—	—	—	—
Lingerie**	12½	14½	16½	18½	20½	22½	24½	26½	28½	30½	32½
	32P	34P	36P	38P	40P	42P	44P	46P	48P	50P	52P
Coats	12½	14½	16½	18½	20½	22½	24½	26½	28½	30½	32½
	—	34P	36P	38P	40P	42P	44P	46P	48P	50P	52P
Suits	12½	14½	16½	18½	20½	22½	24½	26½	28½	30½	32½
Dresses***	12½	14½	16½	18½	20½	22½	24½	26½	28½	30½	32½

* Reprinted courtesy National Retail Merchants Association (NRMA).
** Sweaters, lingerie and intimate apparel—optional sizing to continue as proposed above sizing or 1XP–4XP.
*** Dresses—This size range is identical in fit philosophy to 36–46, not to be confused with traditional Missy sizes 8–20.

VOLUNTARY NOMENCLATURE FOR
WOMEN'S PLUS-SIZE APPAREL*

PROPOSED PLUS-SIZE RANGE	12W	14W	16W	18W	20W	22W	24W	26W	28W	30W	32W
Existing Sizes & Conversions											
Tops	—	34	36	38	40	42	44	46	48	50	52
Bottoms	—	28	30	32	34	36	38	40	42	44	46
Sweaters**	—	34	36	38	40	42	44	46	48	50	52
			1X		2X		3X		4X		
Lingerie**	—	34	36	38	40	42	44	46	48	50	52
			1X / S		2X / M		3X / L		4X / XL		
Coats	—	34	36	38	40	42	44	46	48	50	52
Straight Plus Sizes	—	14	16	18	20	22	24	26	28	30	32
Missy Upgrade	14	16	18	20	22	24	—	—	—	—	—
Suits	—	34	36	38	40	42	44	46	48	50	52
Straight Plus Sizes	—	14	16	18	20	22	24	26	28	30	32
Missy Upgrade	14	16	18	20	22	24	—	—	—	—	—
Dresses***	—	34	36	38	40	42	44	46	48	50	52
Straight Plus Sizes	—	14**	16	18	20	22	24	26	28	30	32
Missy Upgrade	14	16	18	20	22	24	—	—	—	—	—
			1X		2X		3X		4X		

* Reprinted courtesy National Retail Merchants Association (NRMA).

** Sweaters, lingerie and intimate apparel—optional sizing to continue as proposed above sizing or 1XP–4XP.

*** Dresses—This size range is identical in fit philosophy to 36–46, not to be confused with traditional Missy sizes 8–20.

Grading Bodices, Skirts, Sleeves, Pants

The following charts are arranged so that the total grade increase measurement from each pattern size (14 to 24) to the desired sizes up to size 26 is easily read. The measurements are the result of research and data compiled from manufacturers of plus-size women's clothing and the consensus that the ample woman's bust increases in circumference 2 inches per size as she becomes larger. A 2-inch increase, or grade as it is called, is given for sizes 16W through 26W and a 1½-inch grade to sizes 14W and 16W. This is both credible and precise.

Changeable measurements are noted by an asterisk (*). All others are standard.

To read the following charts, find the size of your sample pattern in the first column under **Pattern Size.** Under **Desired Size,** select the size to which you want to increase your pattern to and follow the measurements.

It is important to note that there is no definite agreement among manufacturers on a grading system. Manufacturers have their own grading rules for specific parts of the grade which have proven successful for their target customers.

GRADING BODICES AND SKIRTS

GRADE 1½" = 14W & 16W 2" = 16W–26W		WOMEN'S SIZES: 14W–26W; 14WP–26WP (INCHES)								
PATTERN SIZE	DESIRED SIZE	SHOULDER SLOPE GRADE	NECK GRADE	SHOULDER WIDTH GRADE	ARMHOLE DEPTH GRADE	BUST LEVEL GRADE	SIDE SEAM GRADE	APEX WIDTH GRADE	DART LENGTH GRADE	SKIRT* WAISTLINE & HIP LEVEL GRADE
14	16	⅛	⅛	³⁄₁₆	³⁄₁₆	⅜	⅛	⅛	⅛	⅜
	18	⁵⁄₁₆	¼	⁷⁄₁₆	⅜	⅞	¼	¼	¼	⅞
	20	½	⅜	¹¹⁄₁₆	⁹⁄₁₆	1⅜	⅜	⅜	⅜	1⅜
	22	¹¹⁄₁₆	½	¹⁵⁄₁₆	¾	1⅞	½	½	½	1⅞
	24	⅞	⅝	1³⁄₁₆	¹⁵⁄₁₆	2⅜	⅝	⅝	⅝	2⅜
	26	1¹⁄₁₆	¾	1⁷⁄₁₆	1⅛	2⅞	¾	¾	¾	2⅞
16	18	³⁄₁₆	⅛	¼	³⁄₁₆	½	⅛	⅛	⅛	½
	20	⅜	¼	½	⅜	1	¼	¼	¼	1
	22	⁹⁄₁₆	⅜	¾	⁹⁄₁₆	1½	⅜	⅜	⅜	1½
	24	¾	½	1	¾	2	½	½	½	2
	26	¹⁵⁄₁₆	⅝	1¼	¹⁵⁄₁₆	2½	⅝	⅝	⅝	2½
18	20	³⁄₁₆	⅛	¼	³⁄₁₆	½	⅛	⅛	⅛	½
	22	⅜	¼	½	⅜	1	¼	¼	¼	1
	24	⁹⁄₁₆	⅜	¾	⁹⁄₁₆	1½	⅜	⅜	⅜	1½
	26	¾	½	1	¾	2	½	½	½	2
20	22	³⁄₁₆	⅛	¼	³⁄₁₆	½	⅛	⅛	⅛	½
	24	⅜	¼	½	⅜	1	¼	¼	¼	1
	26	⁹⁄₁₆	⅜	¾	⁹⁄₁₆	1½	⅜	⅜	⅜	1½
22	24	³⁄₁₆	⅛	¼	³⁄₁₆	½	⅛	⅛	⅛	½
	26	⅜	¼	½	⅜	1	¼	¼	¼	1
24	26	³⁄₁₆	⅛	¼	³⁄₁₆	½	⅛	⅛	⅛	½

GRADING SLEEVES

GRADE 1½″ = 14W/WP–16W/WP; 2″ = 16W/WP–26W/WP		WOMEN'S SIZES: 14W–26W; 14WP–26WP				
					(INCHES)	
		CAP HEIGHT GRADE	UNDERARM SEAM, BICEPS TO WRIST GRADE	BICEPS & ELBOW GRADE	WRIST GRADE	
PATTERN SIZE	DESIRED SIZE				STRAIGHT	FITTED
14	16	⅛	¼	½	½	¼
	18	¼	½	1⅛	1⅛	9/16
	20	⅜	¾	1¾	1¾	⅞
	22	½	1	3	3	1½
	24	⅝	1¼	3⅝	3⅝	1 13/16
	26	¾	1½	4¼	4¼	2⅛
16	18	⅛	¼	⅝	⅝	5/16
	20	¼	½	1¼	1¼	⅝
	22	⅜	¾	1⅞	1⅞	15/16
	24	½	1	2½	2½	1¼
	26	⅝	1¼	3⅛	3⅛	1 9/16
18	20	⅛	¼	⅝	⅝	5/16
	22	¼	½	1¼	1¼	⅝
	24	⅜	¾	1⅞	1⅞	15/16
	26	½	1	2½	2½	1¼
20	22	⅛	¼	⅝	⅝	5/16
	24	¼	½	1¼	1¼	⅝
	26	⅜	¾	1⅞	1⅞	15/16
22	24	⅛	¼	⅝	⅝	⅝
	26	¼	½	1¼	1¼	⅝
24	26	⅛	¾	⅝	⅝	5/16

GRADING PANTS						
		WOMEN'S SIZES: 14W–26W; 14WP–26WP				
GRADE 1½" = 14W/WP–16W/WP 2" = 16W/WP–26W/WP		(INCHES)				
PATTERN SIZE	DESIRED SIZE	WAISTLINE & HIP GRADE	CROTCH LENGTH GRADE	CROTCH WIDTH GRADE	INSEAM GRADE	TAPERED ANKLE GRADE
14	16	⅜	¼	⅛	0	³⁄₁₆
	18	⅞	⅝	¼	0	⁷⁄₁₆
	20	1⅜	1	⅜	0	¹¹⁄₁₆
	22	1⅞	1⅜	½	0	¹⁵⁄₁₆
	24	2⅜	1¾	⅝	0	1³⁄₁₆
	26	2⅞	2⅛	¾	0	1⁷⁄₁₆
16	18	½	⅜	⅛	0	¼
	20	1	¾	¼	0	½
	22	1½	1⅛	⅜	0	¾
	24	2	1½	½	0	1
	26	2½	1⅞	⅝	0	1¼
18	20	½	⅜	⅛	0	¼
	22	1	¾	¼	0	½
	24	1½	1⅛	⅜	0	¾
	26	2	1½	¾	0	1
20	22	½	⅜	⅛	0	¼
	24	1	¾	¼	0	½
	26	1½	1⅛	⅜	0	¾
22	24	½	⅜	⅛	0	¼
	26	1	¾	¼	0	½
24	26	½	⅜	⅛	0	¼

How the Plus-Size Body Proportions Increase Per Size

Front & Back Bodice—2" Grade

- The cross shoulder grade is always one-half of the bust grade.

  Example: A 2-inch grade increases the width of each front and back pattern ½-inch, and is referred to as the cross bust grade. The cross shoulder grade is one-half of the cross bust grade or ¼ inch.

- The neck increase appears to be ³⁄₁₆″, but it is actually ⅛″ once the neckline is blended into a smooth curve.

- The ⅛″ increase at the neckline becomes ¹⁄₁₆″ at the armhole to maintain the shoulder slope while grading.

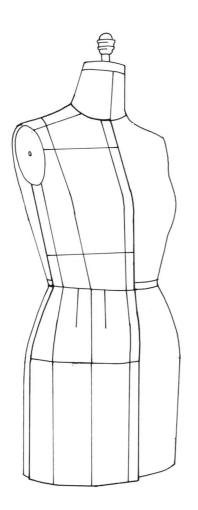

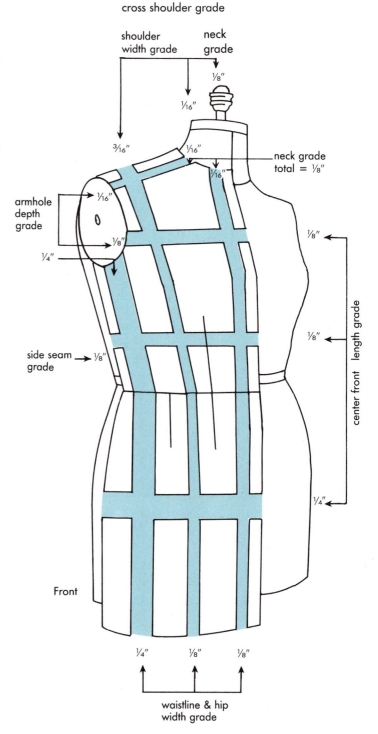

cross shoulder grade

shoulder width grade   neck grade

⅛″

¹⁄₁₆″

³⁄₁₆″   ¹⁄₁₆″

neck grade total = ⅛″

¹⁄₁₆″

armhole depth grade

¹⁄₁₆″

⅛″

¼″

⅛″

⅛″

center front length grade

side seam grade → ⅛″

¼″

Front

¼″   ⅛″   ⅛″

waistline & hip width grade

- The ³⁄₁₆″ increase at the shoulder is distributed at the waistline as ⅛″ on either side of the dart. (The ¹⁄₁₆″ closest to the center front joins the neck increase of ¹⁄₁₆″ to become a ⅛″ increase at the waistline.)

- The armhole increases in depth a standard ³⁄₁₆″ per size, and increases in width a changeable amount equal to one-half of the bust grade.

- The standard apex width grade of ⅛″ per size may also be a changeable amount, equal to one-half of the bust grade or ¼ inch.

- The back bodice grade must be consistent with the front bodice grade.

- The shoulder dart should remain as close to center as possible. Therefore, the ³⁄₁₆″ shoulder increase for the 2″ grade should be divided with ⅛″ placed closest to the neck and the remaining ¹⁄₁₆″ placed on the other side of the dart.

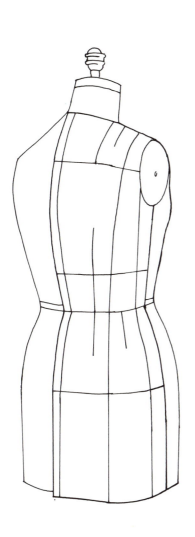

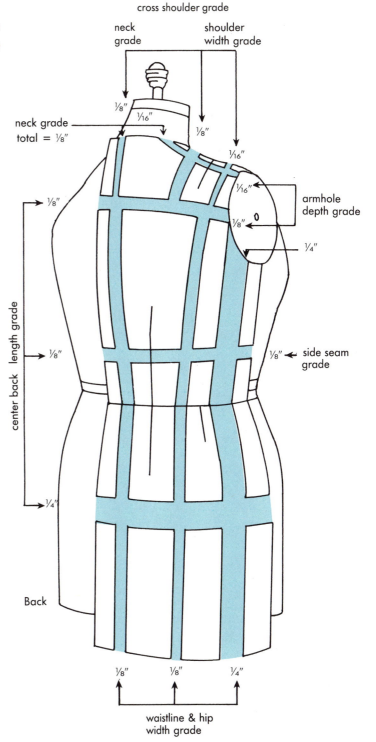

179

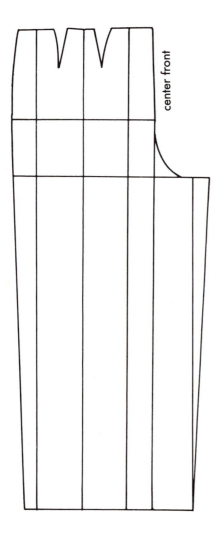

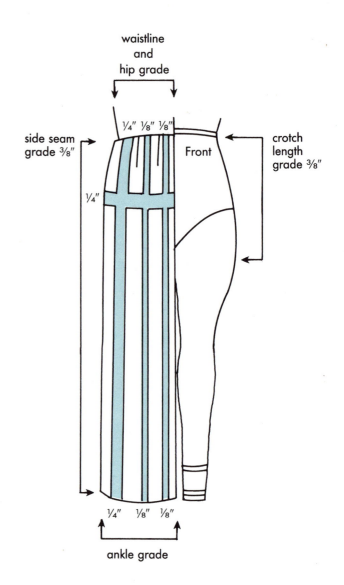

Pants—2" Grade

- The waistline increase is divided equally between the darts as in the basic skirt.

- The crotch is the most important area to consider in order to have proper fit. The crotch length increases ⅜" per size. The crotch width increases ⅛" per size.

- On tapered pants the ankle is always graded one-half of the waistline grade. For example, with a 2" grade the front waistline increases ½", therefore the front ankle increases ¼". On straight slacks, the ankle is graded the same amount as the waist.

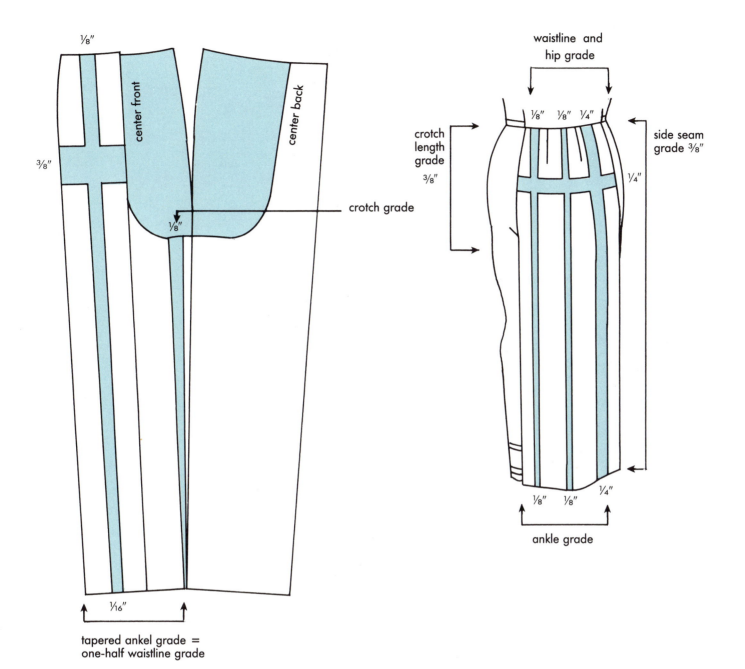

1/8″

center front

center back

3/8″

crotch grade

1/8″

1/16″

tapered ankel grade =
one-half waistline grade

waistline and
hip grade

crotch
length
grade

3/8″

1/8″ 1/8″ 1/4″

side seam
grade 3/8″

1/4″

1/8″ 1/8″

1/4″

ankle grade

Skirt—2″ Grade

- When grading separate skirts—The waistline increase is divided equally between the darts.

- When the skirt is part of a garment—The waistline increase is always the same as that of the bodice waistline, and the distribution of the skirt darts should match the bodice dartlines.

- The total of the width grades widen the waistline, hipline and sweep of the skirt.

- The skirt length may remain the same on women's sizes 14W–18W, and 14WP–18WP. The lengthwise increase of 1/4″ per size is given to sizes 20W–26W and 20WP–26WP.

Sleeve—2″ Grade

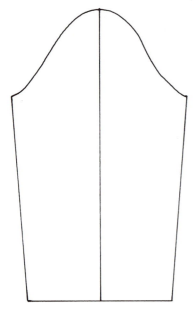

Master Sleeve Sloper

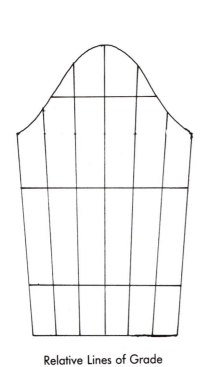

Relative Lines of Grade

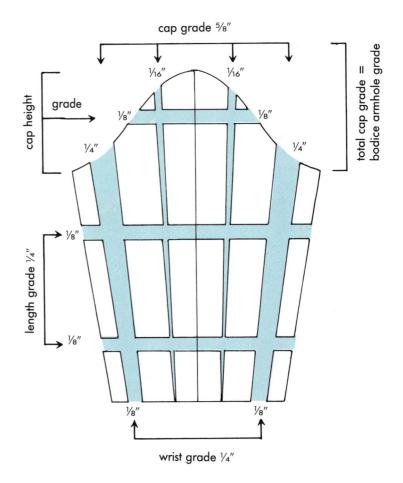

cap grade ⅝″

¹⁄₁₆″   ¹⁄₁₆″

cap height   grade   ⅛″   ⅛″

¼″   ¼″

total cap grade = bodice armhole grade

length grade ¼″   ⅛″

⅛″

⅛″   ⅛″

wrist grade ¼″

Identifying Plus-Size Body Checkpoints

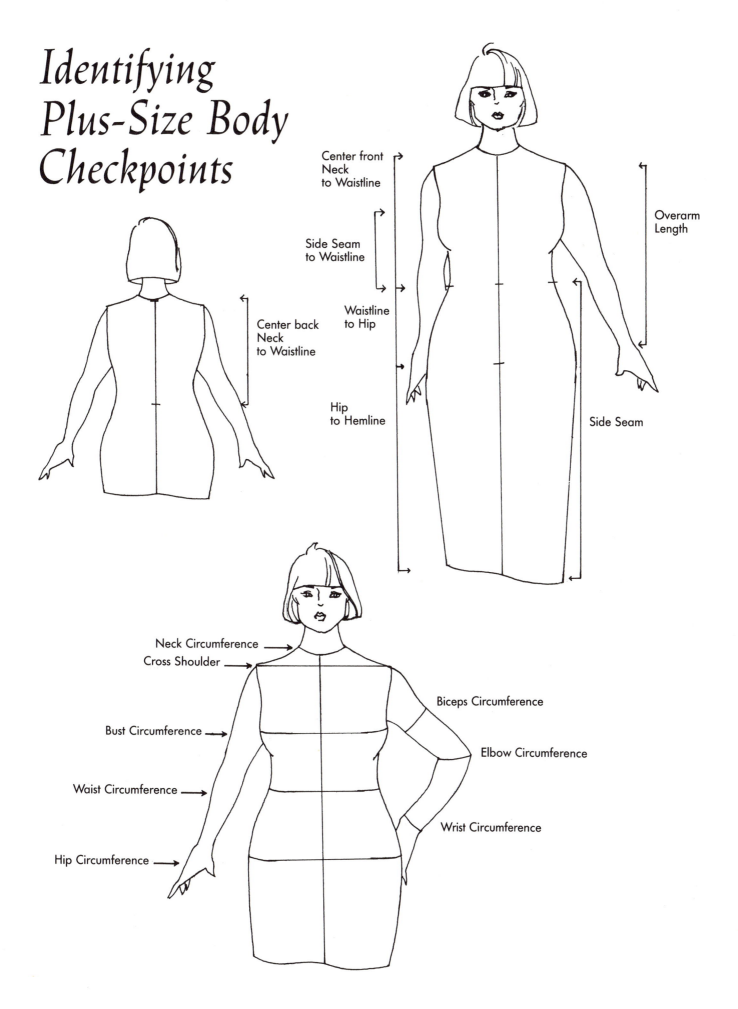

Center front Neck to Waistline

Side Seam to Waistline

Waistline to Hip

Hip to Hemline

Overarm Length

Side Seam

Center back Neck to Waistline

Neck Circumference
Cross Shoulder

Bust Circumference

Waist Circumference

Hip Circumference

Biceps Circumference

Elbow Circumference

Wrist Circumference

Published Sources of Fashion Trends

Color Forecast Services

The following subscription services provide color trends specifically for apparel markets eighteen months in advance of each season. Colors are presented in a series of palettes, and in groups of inspirational combinations.

The Color Association of the United States, 343 Lexington Avenue, New York, N.Y. 10016

The Color Box, Jane Resnick Ltd., 35 West 38 Street, New York, N.Y. 10018

Dixie Yarns Inc., 201 East 17 Street, New York, N.Y. 10003

Pat Tunsky, Inc., 80 West 40 Street, New York, N.Y. 10018

Fiber / Fabric Forecast Services

One of the major benefits fiber companies provide their customers, is color and fabric direction. Ideas and concepts are drawn from all over the world, from the past and present, and are often presented in relation to upcoming silhouettes.

American Cyanamid Co., Fiber Division, 1 Penn Plaza, New York, N.Y. 10001

Anglo Fabrics Co., Inc., 1407 Broadway, New York, N.Y. 10018

Avtex Fibers, Inc., 1185 Avenue of the Americas, New York, N.Y. 10036

Celanese Fibers Operations, Marketing, 1211 Avenue of the Americas, New York, N.Y. 10036

Cone Mills Marketing Co., 1440 Broadway, New York, N.Y. 10018

Cotton Incorporated, 1370 Avenue of the Americas, New York, N.Y. 10019

Courtaulds PLC, 13/14 Margaret Street, London W1A 3DA

Dan River, Inc., 111 West 40 Street, New York, N.Y. 10018

Hoechst Fibers Industries, Creative Service Dept., 1515 Broadway, New York, N.Y. 10036

International Fashion Studio, Wool House, Carlton Gardens, London SW1 Y SAE

Millikin & Co., 1045 Avenue of the Americas, New York, N.Y., 10018

The Wool Bureau, Inc., 360 Lexington Ave., New York, N.Y. 10017

Design Forecast Services

Design forecasting services require an annual subscription and are used by designers, manufacturers and retailers. Since these services are expensive, a manufacturer should investigate them thoroughly before selecting the one that best meets their individual needs. Each of the forecasting services present reports of the basic looks useful for the elaboration of their fashion points in their own individualistic image. They may present their fashion view by design themes and merchandising categories or may provide creative principles useful to the elaboration of new and diversified looks. Each have readily available representatives to clearly explain their service and to solicit new and existing companies as clients.

Listed alphabetically the following are some of the more familiar forecasting services:

Fashion Works, 39 West 38 Street, New York, N.Y. 10018

Here & There, 1412 Broadway, New York, N.Y. 10018

Promostyle, 80 West 40 Street, New York, N.Y. 10016

The Fashion Service, 39 West 38 Street, New York, N.Y. 10018

The Styling Information Services, 154 East 85 Street, New York, N.Y. 10028

Seventeen, 850 Third Avenue, New York, N.Y. 10022

Tobé Report (available to retail stores only), 500 Fifth Avenue, New York, N.Y. 10110

Trade News Publications

Women's Wear Daily (WWD), Fairchild Publications, 7 East 12 Street, New York, N.Y. 10003. The most important trade newspaper for women's apparel. All the needed news on the business of fashion published daily and includes supplements that periodically explore the latest trends in the plus-size business.

W (published weekly by the same publishers of *Women's Wear Daily)*. It covers reprints of "soft" news (interviews with personalities, fashion reports, society news and so on covered during the week in *WWD*. Included are manufacturers and retailers' ads not carried in the daily paper.

California Apparel News, California Fashion Publications, 945 South Wall Street, Los Angeles, California 90015. A weekly publication that covers the West Coast markets.

Fashion Showcase, 1145 Empire Central Place, Suite 100, Dallas, Texas 75247. Its focus is commercial fashion in Texas and midwestern states.

Western Apparel Industry, 112 West 9th Street, Los Angeles, California 90015. Trade developments and innovations with a West Coast perspective.

American Fabrics and Fashions, 343 Lexington Avenue, New York, N.Y. 10016. Published by Bobbin International six times a year in a full color format that addresses fabric as one part of the fashion pipeline. Full color actual size fabric swatches are included.

Fabric News to the Trade, 21 East 40 Street, New York, N.Y. 10016. A directory to New York textile firms and industry news.

Stores, 100 West 31 Street, New York, N.Y. 10001. A trade magazine for retail stores.

Women's Large and Half Size Specialty Stores, Salesman's Guide, Inc., 1140 Broadway, New York, N.Y. 10001. A nationwide directory.

PS The Business of Special Sizes. Earnshaw Publications, 225 West 34 Street, Suite 1212, New York, N.Y. 10122. *PS* is the business publication of the plus-size market. *PS'* charter issue arrived October 1, 1987. Published six times a year.

Maxima Magazine, Maxima Publications, Inc., P.O. Box 090181, Birmingham, Michigan 48009. A magazine for the plus-size woman published quarterly. Premier issue published fall 1987.

Foreign Fashion Publications

Belezza. Aldo Palazzi Editore, Via Zuretti 37, Milan, Italy, Italian high fashion.

Calze Moda Maglie. Calze Moda Maglia, SES, Co., S1, Magenta 32, Milan, Italy. European knitwear, especially Italian.

Chic. Ross Verlag, Spinchernstr. 12, 5 Cologne, West Germany. German fashions.

Elle. 6 rue Ancello, 92521 Neuille, France. Published weekly. This is one of the most influential junior French lifestyle publications.

Grazia. Published by Arnoldo Mondadori, Editore, 20090 Segrate, Milan, Italy. Trendy junior design.

Harper's and **Queen.** Chestergate House, Vauxhall Bridge Road, London SW1, England, British version of *Harper's Bazaar.*

Harper's Bazaar (Italia). Corso di Porta Nuova, 46 Milan, Italy. Italian edition of *Harper's Bazaar.*

Linea Italiana. Mondadori Publishing, 437 Madison Avenue, New York, N.Y. 10022. High fashion women's wear. Also publishes *Linea Italiana Uomo* for men's wear.

Marie Claire and 100 Ideas. 11 bis, rue Boissyd' Anglas, 75008 Paris, France. Influential magazines covering junior fashions and lifestyles.

Officiel de la Couture et de la Mode de Paris. Officiel de la Couture SA, 226 Rue du Faubourg St. Honore, Paris 8e, France. Most important couture publication, published quarterly.

Officiel du Prêt-à-Porter. Societe Europeane d'Edition et de Publicite, 265 Avenue Louise, 1050 Brussels, Belgium.

Style. 481 University Avenue, Toronto, Ontario M5W1A7, Canada. Fashions in Canada.

Ultima Moda. Mexican report on domestic and foreign high fashion.

Vogue. Published in France, England, Italy, and Australia. Each edition covers domestic fashion for that country plus foreign styles. Special editions cover men's wear and active sports that influence fashions, like *Uomo Vogue* and *Vogue Mare* in Italy and *Vogue Homme* in France.

Index

INDEX